Emotional Impact

Emotional Impact

Passionate leaders and corporate transformation

Philip Channer

and

Tina Hope

palgrave

First published 2001 by
PALGRAVE
Houndmills, Basingstoke, Hampshire RG21 6XS and
175 Fifth Avenue, New York, N.Y. 10010
Companies and representatives throughout the world

PALGRAVE is the new global academic imprint of
St. Martin's Press LLC Scholarly and Reference Division and
Palgrave Publishers Ltd (formerly Macmillan Press Ltd).

ISBN 0–333–92547–5 hardback

This book is printed on paper suitable for recycling and made from fully managed and sustained forest sources.

A catalogue record for this book is available from the British Library.

Editing and origination by
Aardvark Editorial, Mendham, Suffolk

10 9 8 7 6 5 4 3 2 1
10 09 08 07 06 05 04 03 02 01

Printed and bound in Great Britain by
Creative Print & Design (Wales), Ebbw Vale

Contents

PART II

PART III

Foreword

This book is about leadership. In particular about some of the harder-to-define parts – the connection between leadership and what it feels like to be a leader. We are trying to capture and communicate what it feels like to be responsible for leading, and changing, an organisation, whether it consists of ten or tens of thousands of people.

The book was inspired by the fact that most accounts written by, or about, leaders, even those who have led organisations through turbulence and change, say little, if anything, about what it was like for them as a person, as though that aspect was unimportant. This conflicts with our experience as consultants and coaches to business leaders, which is that it is the emotional competencies – from empathy through to resilience – which really distinguish the transformational leader.

To put this book into context, leadership is now a much researched topic, often to the theme that 'the world needs better leaders'. Many models and theories have been developed in pursuit of a philosopher's stone. Similarly, emotional intelligence is now also a hot management topic.

However, this book is not intended as a piece of research, nor as the basis for a new theory, nor to provide some sort of foolproof set of recipes for success. Rather, it is intended to strengthen the argument that we should be more emotionally literate in business – that we should be more open to, and about, the whole topic of the emotions.

By getting several well-known business people to describe their change leadership experiences, we are hoping to shine a light into what has hitherto been a rather dark corner of leadership – the way in which the human challenge of change has impacted those responsible for leading it.

If nothing else, the openness shown by the individuals whose stories are told here may encourage others to be similarly open. Our thanks are primarily to them.

Prologue: Our Theme

> Most executives have a notoriously underdeveloped capacity for understanding and dealing with emotions. (Harry Levinson)[1]

Traditional analyses of what makes a successful business leader, as well as the personal accounts of the leaders themselves, have understated the importance of the part played by a leader's ability to connect to, and manage, both their own feelings and those of the people in the organisation. Our experience, however, is that sensitivity, both to their own emotions and to those of others, is an essential competence for any business leader, particularly one who seeks to change an organisation, since this requires winning hearts as well as minds.

Historically, there has been a heavy concentration on a leader's rational, cognitive capabilities, but actually it takes much more than this. The burden of introducing 'softer' skills falls on the leader, which, in turn, requires the leader to be able to exercise their own skills in this area. In other words, since the role of the leader is to bring into play all the capabilities – not just the rational ones – of the people in the organisation, the first step they have to be able to take is to do the same thing for themselves.

The stories in this book illustrate, therefore, how a number of leaders have used personal transformation and mastery of their own feelings to drive organisational transformation. In the past not much has been said on this topic. One of the main reasons that the emotional aspects of leadership have hitherto been overlooked is that, until recently, leaders themselves, with few notable exceptions, have rarely talked about their emotions, about how they feel, and have felt. At least they have not talked openly to their colleagues, or in any sort of public forum. If we took at face value their own accounts of their achievements, the emotional side of things – what the experience really was like for them, how they felt, what they had to endure – was of little significance. It cannot have been that they did not experience strong feelings. There is no reason to suppose that they are not as affected by emotion as the rest of us.

Their reticence may have reflected the prevailing attitude in society that it is 'not done' to air such matters, or, that as men, since almost all leaders are still men, they felt that the emotions are best left in John Gray's

Martian cave where they had experienced them.[2] However, the most likely reason is that there has been in the past a positive pressure from business organisations to shun anything to do with the emotional. As Tichy and Sherman wrote in 1993:[3]

Most organisations don't know how to deal with emotion, so they try to pretend it doesn't exist. By design, corporations seem emotionally barren. Feelings, one understands, are best expressed at home, where they won't gum up the machinery of scientific management. The emotional sterility of the business environment is a cordon sanitaire around the fear, jealousy, resentment, rage, longing, pride, ambition, and God-knows-what-else that seethe in human hearts.

It is not just that in large companies the traditional qualities required of a leader originally mirrored the model of scientific management – which was hierarchical, bureaucratic, control-focused, and, above all, cognitive. It's that, as the antithesis of rationality, emotions are seen by business as a threat, rather than a potentially valuable support to be harnessed. The consequence is that only a limited range of emotional expression tends to be socially acceptable (that is, not negative emotions such as fear, anxiety, anger), and organisations have developed what Ashford and Humphrey[4] identify as a number of means of controlling or suppressing their expression.

Emotions have, therefore, been seen as a positive threat to an orderly, militaristic world. They confused the issue, undermined authority, complicated planning, and interfered with good judgement.[5] To experience emotions, let alone to admit them, could, therefore, be career-threatening. What's more, the higher you climb in an organisation the more visible you are. Which has the corollary that the more pressure you come under, the less open you can be about how you really do feel with anyone inside the organisation – boss, peer, or subordinate is equally out of reach. But now there are fewer taboos. With increased research into the role that emotions play in our lives, and the current popularisation of emotional intelligence as a management topic, there is an opportunity to change this paradigm.

Awareness of the part played by emotions in all aspects of our lives, including our business lives, has been stimulated by authors such as Goleman and Cooper and by practitioner/academics such as Manfred Kets de Vries. And business does reflect society, where recognition of the importance of our inner lives is growing, if only in reaction to the current epidemic of stress. And there are fewer and fewer areas of personal experience that cannot be openly discussed.

We believe that there are several good reasons for focusing on the human aspects of leadership quite apart from helping future leaders to understand what it takes to succeed.

The most immediate is to undermine the myth that, because of the risks inherent in negative emotions such as anger and jealousy, the whole topic of the emotions has no place in the world of business. This may make individuals either suppress their emotional self-awareness, or feel weak, guilty, or inadequate if they fail so to do.

There are several benefits, both for themselves and others, if business leaders are able to be more open about what it is really like to be in such a position – both the joys and the stresses. As powerful role models they will 'make it OK' for others to develop their own emotional competence, and to take their own emotional well-being seriously.

Although we have included a section at the end of this book on developing our human side, we do not seek to provide any answers, beyond the most simplistic. Whatever the self-help books may say, the reality is that no quick and easy route exists for any of us to self-awareness. Emotional intelligence cannot be gained from a checklist, and a number of other characteristics are required for success, since life will always be tough for leaders, as Sir John Harvey-Jones recognised (although he was not specifically talking about emotional toughness):

> The prime characteristic I have detected in top leaders is toughness. There is no doubt that these jobs are immensely demanding of time, concentration, sheer grinding brain power and the ability to live an intrinsically unhealthy existence.[6]

How this book is organised

We felt that the best way of sharing an understanding of 'what it takes' in emotional terms to lead large organisations was to interview a number of individuals who have themselves led organisations, sometimes through significant change, and let them tell their own stories as directly as possible. Most of this book, and by far the most vital part, consists of these accounts which we have recorded from interviews and which have been reviewed by the interviewees. In order to provide the context, we have prefaced each account with some background information on the organisation and the individual. However, before setting out the individual stories we thought it would be helpful first to explore briefly the background to the whole question of leadership and emotions, and to set out more clearly why it is that we believe that these accounts are valuable.

So in Part I we look at questions such as 'What are the traditional and evolving models of leadership?' 'What does it take to manage change?' 'To what extent do leadership models recognise the importance of emotional competence?' The second part consists of the stories. Part III summarises the themes that come out of the individual interviews, and then looks at how the context for leadership is changing. What will be the impact of any changes in society's attitude towards the emotional content of our work, and what new challenges will the evolving forms of organisation present? Lastly we consider briefly the sort of things that a leader might consider doing to develop their human side.

Part I

Part I

1 Summary of the Myths

The idea for this book came from our experience of working with leaders who had been responsible for, and successful in, delivering transformational change. In working with these individuals, it seemed obvious to us that there was something extraordinary about them, and this 'specialness' seemed to us different from the media-created image of such leaders. Therefore it seemed important to lay out some of the myths that surround the whole subject of leadership and of change. In Chapter 11 we revisit these to see what perspective our sample gives us on this.

The myth of the leader as superhero

Typically, in much of the media, these leaders are portrayed as 'super-heroes' who can leap tall buildings in a single bound. The impression is that these individuals are somehow superhuman and therefore, by definition, different from the rest of us. This impression both jarred and contrasted strongly with our personal experience of these individuals. In working with them they typically came across as warmly human, charismatic undoubtedly, but clearly subject to, and experiencing, the same roller-coaster of excitement, fears, doubts and joys as the rest of us. Nor did it seem to us that their achievements made things necessarily any easier for them, or that the successful delivery of these extraordinary achievements had no less of an impact on them emotionally. To our eyes, their specialness was much more rooted in their ability to see beyond the difficulties and 'go for it' anyway. Their focus on the end goal, and not on the journey, equipped them to cope better with the difficulties that lay ahead. We believe this perspective provides a different slant to the debate on the leadership of change.

The leader as grandmaster

Many of the discussions and profiles of the leaders of change often create the impression that these individuals are a unique breed, with inherent qualities which fundamentally differentiate them from the rest of us, and that, by dint of who and what they are, they are able to cause vast organisations to undergo change.

The impression is that leaders sit apart from the change, that their involvement is an entirely rational one without any real personal impact on them as individuals. The leaders are positioned 'above' the organisation and the change, directing things from afar, concerned solely with the rational moves that must be made in pursuance of the future – as though they are skilled and logical grandmasters playing a game of corporate chess.

At the same time, by virtue of their position and skills, they are perceived as being smarter in dealing with the political dimensions of change than others in the organisation, and are thus able to effortlessly orchestrate and manage the political (that is, power) shifts that are inevitably a consequence of the change.

Any recognition, and it is a rare recognition, of a more personal involvement in a change acknowledges the isolation of leaders and concludes that, given this position, they are potentially more prone to stress and therefore more likely to derail as a consequence of their involvement.

In contrast, our experience highlights these individuals as deeply human, having the same fears and concerns as the rest of us. Furthermore, they have a strong concern for the people in the organisation, and work hard in thinking how best to engage them in any change. Their involvement in the change is deeply personal.

The myth of change as being new

Change is continually talked about these days. The rate of change is accelerating and is now an accepted part of everyday life. However, the impression is that this phenomenon of change is entirely new, and that as a result people are expected to cope with an entirely new set of skills. The future is painted as being far more difficult than the past, with all the key elements of an individual's work life being fundamentally different.

Our experience most certainly confirms that there is an unprecedented increase in the pace of change. But while we believe that the future will, without doubt, be different from the past, we do not believe that it will necessarily be more difficult to cope with – it will just be different.

The myth that we are different in the workplace to who we are at home

The business of management is still largely discussed and taught as if management was a science, with the implicit belief that most significant management issues can be analysed, understood and resolved from a rational perspective. This view largely ignores human nature, and implies that the reactions, feelings and behaviours of individuals at work are somehow different from those they experience and exhibit in the rest of their life.

This myth tends to reinforce the belief that organisational life is conducted on a rational basis, with most of the 'non-rational' energy being employed in understanding the 'political dimensions' of an organisation.

Comparatively little teaching (other than specialised human resource interventions) is devoted to discussing or thinking through the management of the more human, or indeed emotional, side of work – that is, how individuals react to issues that impact them personally in the business environment.

Our experience, however, tends to confirm Tichy and Sherman's observation that 'work, inevitably, is an emotional experience; healthy people can't just drop their feelings off at home like a set of golf clubs'.[1]

The myth of emotional gender difference

It is fashionable for (generally male) observers to hold out great hopes of the ability of women leaders to improve the human condition. For example, Warren Bennis[2] says: 'the US's competitive advantage will be the leadership of women', a hope based on the assumption that women can bring to business a new dimension of caring and sensitivity that is derived from their own greater emotional capabilities.

There is some evidence, summarised in Dianne Hales' book *Just Like a Woman*,[3] of some gender differences – for example, in the way that men and women express anger. However, it is not possible to conclude that men and women feel all emotions differently, or that the differences in the way they express them are anything but cultural.

All of these myths, which contain at least a grain of truth, form part of the background against which organisational transformation takes place.

We tried to bear them in mind while carrying out our interviews and in pulling together our observations in Chapter 11.

In this way, we try to refocus the balance from the purely rational to what we see as the more realistically human dimension. It is our strong belief that it is *the narrative truth which is the most important dimension of reality*. This clearly has as many aspects as the number of individuals involved in a change. (In the next section we highlight this from the perspective of the leader.)

2 Leadership Theories

Leadership is like beauty: it's hard to define, but you know it when you see it.[1]

Leadership is now a much-studied, much-defined and much-taught subject. By the mid-1990s Manfred Kets de Vries[2] had already identified 70 published definitions of leadership, and there are no doubt more by now. In fact, according to Van Seters and Field[3] we are already in at least the ninth identifiable era of thinking about leadership, which started with the great man theories, and continues today with transformational leadership – the leader as change agent. Perhaps unsurprisingly, the volume of study has not produced the same amount of clarity – Bennis and Nanus, who have contributed more than most to our understanding of leadership, say 'leadership is the most studied and least understood topic of any in the social sciences'.[4]

Why is there such interest?

Why there is so much interest in what it takes to be an effective leader deserves a little study in itself. It indicates the importance that is attached to the role, and the weight of the expectations laid upon it. It may, as Kets de Vries suggests, be driven by some deep-felt need for 'a beacon in an era of change'[5] – a subconscious search for the perfect parent figure.

It may also be driven by the very practical issue organisations now face that, however many millions of dollars they throw at management education and development, the perceived task of leadership has got bigger and more challenging over the years. Deconstructing it into bite-sized chunks makes it look less daunting; and writing it down makes it seem more under control, more capable of being mastered.

Whatever the cause, observers and researchers have been prolific at coming up with analyses of what it takes to be an effective leader. It is as though listing the ingredients, or photographing it from many angles, is an adequate description of a cake, when in fact it's the combination of the undefined intangibles – taste, texture, smell, appearance – that make the cake special.

Leadership theories

Over the years, leadership has been analysed from a number of different angles. Thinking and research has looked at, among other things: the ideal traits of a leader; what leaders actually do; leadership styles; how different situations demand different sorts of skills and qualities; and the critical relationship between the leader and the followers.

It is not the purpose of this book to track through the labyrinth of how thinking progressed from one era to another (Sadler[6] does a user-friendly job of this), but more to look for signs that leadership theory recognises the part played by the emotions as well as all the other capabilities.

Scientific management

One of the favourite ways of looking at leadership is to list all the desirable traits of a leader. Originally these lists focused on what are now seen as basic skills. Earlier this century the first large-scale industrial organisations were being created, and the emphasis was on designing and operating these new businesses in a quasi-engineering sense, – on 'managing' them – as though the natural energies thereby pooled were some sort of volatile force that had to be contained lest they run out of control, or else they had to be carefully channelled and husbanded to create efficiencies.

Frederick Taylor's scientific management, therefore, required managers who had an entirely rational set of abilities – to plan and budget, organise and staff, control and problem-solve.

Leadership versus management

As leadership began to be distinguished from management, the emotions were clearly one dimension in which they might differ. Thus for Zaleznik in *Managers and Leaders are they Different?*[7], leaders relate to people in a way that is more intuitive and emotional, and convey a more personal vision through images that excite and inspire.

Or, as John Kotter[8] puts it: where the manager plans and budgets, the leader establishes direction; where the manager organises and staffs, the leader aligns people; where the manager controls and problem-solves, the leader motivates and inspires.

In terms of capability, therefore, the manager has to be equipped to handle tactics and structure, the 'how' of the business. The leader, on the other hand, has to be able to create the vision, inspire and energise his or her people towards the 'what'.

Charismatic and transformational leadership

There are varying accounts of charismatic or transformational leadership, which particularly focus on the role of the leader as change agent. These accentuate the emotional aspects of leadership. For example, Tichy and Devanna[9] included courage and the ability to cope with ambiguity and uncertainty among the characteristics they observed in a study of transformational leaders.

At times the manager versus leader debate seems to be something of a false dichotomy. As Kets de Vries[10] says, we would really like our leaders to be both:

> Looking at effective leaders we can distinguish between two roles, both necessary. One is charismatic; the other, instrumental. Leaders need to envision the future and empower, energise, and motivate their followers. But leaders also have to structure, design, control, and reward behaviour.

But how easy is it for one person to do both? The challenge of being able to fulfil both roles remains, and is one that the would-be leader has to meet at a very deep, personal level. Zaleznik[11] describes it as follows:

> A crucial difference between managers and leaders lies in the conceptions they hold, deep in their psyches, of chaos and order. Leaders tolerate chaos and lack of structure... Managers seek order and control.

Traditional leadership theory is, therefore, beginning to recognise the part played by the emotions when the leader has to be charismatic, to win hearts and minds in order to make change happen, and to demonstrate tenacity. But it is still a rather limited emotional repertoire that is being described.

3 Managing Change

Change is threatening

Change is inevitable, natural and a part of life. According to most commentators and, indeed, to observable experience, change is happening more and more rapidly. This rate of change will continue to increase as we move through the early part of this new millennium. Often we talk about this acceleration as exciting and challenging, yet when it impacts us on a personal basis change can be, and is, hugely threatening. Change by definition means letting go of what we have previously done or held on to; it means doing something different. Undertaking a new challenge requires faith, courage, insight and resilience. It can often mean stepping off a precipice into the unknown.

Most people fear change

Given this background, and the potential for stress and emotional challenge that change poses, it is not surprising that most people do not, when it comes to it, actually like change or relish the prospect of it. Many people talk about change in theory, and about their desire for it in all or part of their lives, yet when it comes to the crunch very few individuals proactively or willingly embrace change.

There are, of course, the exceptions, and it is true that for all sorts of reasons some people at some time in their lives welcome the opportunity to be different or to do things differently. Even then most of these individuals are reacting to some kind of external stimuli. The process of initiating and driving through change, particularly when it has to involve and engage a number of people, is very different and poses a completely different scale of challenge. It takes a special individual to drive and undertake such change.

Reactive change

Responding to the need for change, and aligning an organisation to follow through a given path, has traditionally been the remit of those who have

10

headed organisations. Yet many changes undertaken by organisations have either been relatively minor in scale or have been rendered necessary or inevitable by changes in the environment (for example technology, competition or regulation). These 'reactive' changes are not the kind of changes or the kind of leaders we had in mind when putting together this text.

Proactive leaders of change

We have been talking to the type of leader who, independently and ahead of any 'required' changes, sat down and developed a new vision as to how their business or industry could look; who then planned and built the momentum within their organisation for driving towards this new future, and followed through the implementation. This is a very different type of leader. The proactive transformations that these individuals have led are typically different in scale, impact and sustainability, and are much rarer than those brought about reactively.

Yet the emotional impact of the change on the individual is not fundamentally different, varying with neither the catalyst nor the actuality. What is arguably different is the willingness and motivation for such individuals to embrace change – this is one of the things that set them apart. We will look at this in more detail in the final section of this book.

The process of change

Change, whatever the scale or motivation, is a recognisable management process and much has been written about it. Individuals and organisations that undergo or experience change pass through an emotional cycle with identifiable elements and stages. This 'emotional cycle of change' was identified and annotated by Kurt Lewin. In our experience, this model best describes the cycle of emotions that an organisation goes through, on an individual and collective basis, when experiencing change.

The model maps and characterises the reactions and emotions that are typically experienced and observed once a change initiative is under way. It assumes that the decision for change has already been made, and that the first steps of the programme have been taken. In other words, it assumes that a 'burning platform' is already in place, and that the process of change has begun.

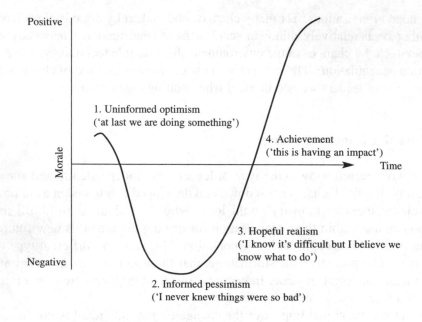

Figure 3.1   Lewin change model

The initiation of change

This model does not discuss the initiation of change. As intimated above, change can be, and often is, a reactive move on the part of organisations to respond to external stimuli. When this is the case, the reasons for change are clearly rational and explainable. The change is often expected, or seen as overdue, by the organisation, ahead of any announcement or specific action. This type of rational, incremental change is often finally triggered as the result of a researched and reasoned collective decision taken by the board, with the accompanying message and subsequent programme of actions then being cascaded down through the organisation.

Initiating transformational change – the vision

At other times, and typically when transformational change is envisaged, the trigger upfront is entirely different. In such circumstances, the change is likely to begin with a vision, a picture as to how an organisation might look different in the future in order to fit it for significantly improved competitive advantage. The process often begins as an ambition, for example 'to be the number one airline' or 'to fundamentally reshape the nature of the customer relationship'.

This vision is usually, but not always, the dream of a single individual. It can be the result of reasoned research, but more typically starts with an individual, most probably the chief executive, who has an ambition for the business. This is often tied in with the career ambition of the chief executive. (We will examine this in more depth later.)

It is our experience that a chief executive is likely to initiate significant change at one of two points during their tenure. This may either be early in their role, when they are still somewhat at a distance from the day-to-day running of the business and are unencumbered by many of the existing barriers. Or it may come towards the end of their tenure when they are seeking to embed their legacy. Clearly this is not true of all chief executives, since the number to have this kind of major impact is few and far between. We look at the experiences of some who have achieved such change in Part II.

Change engenders an emotional reaction

Whatever the trigger for change, once it is under way, it, perhaps more than anything else, throws into question the precept that management's and the individual's behaviour at work are rational, and that we are all rational people. Change strikes right at the heart – and engenders an emotional reaction. Perhaps uniquely in what happens in the workplace, change blurs the line between who we want to be at work, and who we really are as a human being. Thus, change is a process which is more 'real-life' than almost any other process that happens in business.

Change issues thus throw up significant human stories, and it is these that we have sought to understand during the course of this work.

However, in laying out the framework, the Lewin emotional cycle is an extremely valuable tool.

The start-up of change

Once a change initiative has begun, the start-up is typically a time of huge excitement and energy, characterised by a feeling of 'at last something is happening'. This is the time when an organisation is, as it were, getting its act together. Although there is a lot of activity, there is little real action.

The organisation and the individuals within it are seeking to assure themselves that they have made the right decision to go ahead. No actual changes are as yet happening.

The dawning of reality

Once the initial commotion around the start-up is over, organisations typically seek to analyse where they are, to understand the reality of the situation they are in, and to plan out the scale of the journey they are to undertake. It is at this stage that the enormity of the task facing the organisation becomes apparent, and the individuals involved in the change gain an insight into what is expected of them in the new order. It is at this stage that the reality that things will be different from now on begins to hit home and consequently organisations and individuals alike experience a drop in morale.

Defensive reactions

This stage of the journey can be characterised by 'I never knew things were so bad'. The early excitement dissipates, people begin clinging on to the good old days, and reasons are found as to why either the change may not really be necessary, or why the analysis being undertaken is inaccurate. There is now a strong risk of 'analysis paralysis'; organisations and their change efforts often get bogged down into increasingly detailed and irrelevant analysis.

The need for leadership

Change initiatives often fail at this point. Leadership is the critical driver in moving things beyond this low point. Leaders have a role in 'holding the mirror up', warts and all, to the organisation. The task is to gain broad acceptance to the picture that is reflected.

Planning the way ahead

It is not necessary to have all the i's dotted or t's crossed in the plan, indeed, as indicated above, this can be counter-productive.

The challenge is in gathering sufficient data in order to understand in broad terms the necessary length, direction and impact of the subsequent journey. Confidence must be built, both at an organisational and individual level, that the current situation is not sustainable, that change is inevitable, and that it will result in significant advantage.

In order for everyone to understand what is required of them, it is necessary to plan the likely steps and milestones of the journey towards the future in adequate, but not binding, detail. If successful, at this stage the organisational morale will be characterised by 'now I understand... I can see the way forward... I know what is expected of me'. This is the most critical stage in ensuring a successful transformation.

Sustaining enthusiasm

Once the inevitability of change has been instilled into the organisation, and excitement has been built about the forthcoming journey, the challenge then shifts to engaging people's enthusiasm for sustaining the implementation. It is important to achieve small successes, and to celebrate those successes, in order to demonstrate that the end goal is achievable, and that people can make a difference. The response one is seeking is 'now I know we can do it'.

The cycle of emotions

This cycle of emotions is repeated time and again throughout a change initiative. The depths and heights of the emotional reaction depend on the pace and scale of the change, and on the skill of the leadership team in driving towards the end point. Individuals also tend to go through the cycle at different times, depending on the directness with which any element of the programme impacts on them. As change begins to effect an individual personally, it starts to expose private motives and personal agendas and can be stressful.

The leadership team during change

Successful change happens when the leadership team is able to predict in advance the coming shifts in morale and makes plans to mitigate them. Skilful management is the most critical lever in driving through change.

But of course the leadership team itself goes through the emotional cycle and needs to secure support for itself to ensure it stays on track. Leaders, who carry the personal responsibility for change, have to cope with the emotional ups and downs, and it is often during change programmes that they find themselves at their most exposed.

Ongoing change

If an organisation successfully negotiates the emotional cycle, it will achieve significant progress against its end target. It will also have a sustainable improvement in its ability to cope with change. Since change is not a one-off event, but rather an ongoing process, the ability to cope with it is a significant competitive tool and one worthy of nurturing.

The human element is key to successful change

Yet in planning change, organisations traditionally have focused on the task management elements, that is they have identified in substantial detail the steps that must be taken to move the business from where it is now to where it wishes to be. Many organisations have an impressive capability in planning, and it is not unusual to walk into a 'corporate war room' which is plastered with Gantt charts showing the sequence of events and the milestones to be reached on the way to the change. In addition many organisations increasingly have change departments whose responsibility it is to handle these events.

However, despite this activity, most change initiatives, particularly those of a transformational nature, tend to fail. This is largely because organisations ignore or fail to prioritise the need to focus on the human side of change. By failing to give appropriate recognition to the likely impact on individuals of asking them to do something different, they tend to sub-optimise the business results deliverable from significant change.

Involvement is critical

In order to overcome the inherent stress in change, an investment must be made in involving the individuals affected. This requires helping them to understand the reasons for the change and then, as appropriate, getting them involved in how best to make the journey towards the end point.

While the upfront investment in time to achieve this is significant, such mobilisation through involvement reaps benefits downstream in terms of morale and enthusiasm.

The rational, emotional and political dimensions

Change management means understanding the likely impact and sequence of the change on all three dimensions – rational (what needs to be done, when, how and by whom); political (how will it impact on the status quo); and emotional (how will it impact emotionally, individually and collectively across the organisation). Guiding an organisation along a transformational journey demands the ability to recognise where, on all three dimensions, the business is, and then to be able to design interventions, and manage communications and behaviours accordingly.

Engaging the hearts and minds

While a number of the tasks can be managed effectively from a task perspective, success fundamentally depends on engaging the 'hearts and minds' of the people in the business. It is certain that any change will generate 'winners and losers' when comparing the future state against the present. It is clearly much easier to harness the enthusiasm and involvement of those who stand to win. There is no easy way of managing 'losers'; they will find it extremely difficult to 'buy-in' emotionally to the need for change and the inevitable result. Therefore, investing time and energy in persuading them may prove fruitless. The best that can be hoped for is that a fair process is followed so that they feel they have been treated fairly, even if they do not agree with the outcome. A process that is felt to be fair also helps to minimise any impact of 'survivor syndrome' on the remainder of the organisation.

Leadership and change

The need to handle all the multifarious requirements of change places a unique strain on the leadership of the business. Ultimately success can only be driven top down. While a leadership team has a huge responsibility for managing the success of the change through communication, championing and role modelling, at the end of the day the final accountability lies with the leader who envisaged and catalysed the initiative.

4 Transformational Leadership

The old command-and-control hierarchies and 'scientific' management have had to give way to a new, devolved and empowered way of running a business simply to survive in what has become a much more fast-moving and competitive world.

Management has thus evolved into leadership, in some cases truly transformational in nature. While there might have been some doubt earlier as to the difference between managing and leading, transformational leaders are clearly doing more than just maintaining the status quo or even creating incremental change. They are taking their organisations through step changes.

What happens in a business transformation?

According to consultants Gouillart and Kelly[1], the transformation of a business, which 'is now the central management challenge and the primary, if not the sole, task of business leaders' is 'the orchestrated redesign of the genetic architecture of the corporation'. In other words, a dramatic rearrangement of the DNA of the whole system.

The transformational leader's task is thus the regeneration, over time, of all aspects of a business. This can involve, as we have seen, redefining the vision, through restructuring where necessary, to the creation of new businesses, and the putting in place of the people, organisation structures, processes and systems to make it work.

Not all transformation programmes are of the same scale as General Electric, where by 1996 Jack Welch had presided over acquisitions or disposals of 819 businesses worth a combined $69 billion.

At an individual business unit level, a transformation programme is likely to impact, directly or indirectly, 60–80 per cent of the employees: redesigning the way they work through process reengineering; removing layers of management and making them more visible and accountable;

providing better information flows; or improving teamwork, within and across departments.

Of course, all of this is highly disruptive while the changes are being designed and implemented. Once the programme is rolling, people get carried away with enthusiasm – in one organisation, where we ran a two-year programme to improve the effectiveness of an oil and gas exploration and production company, at one point no less than 42 per cent of the staff were involved directly in the project. The managing director had to come to the project team to borrow his staff back when other critical duties arose.

The role of the leader during transformation

Descriptions of business transformations may not excite the emotions when read in cold print, but when experienced in real life they can feel heart-stoppingly challenging if you are responsible for leading them. Partly through sheer scale and complexity – for example, do you reorganise first and then reengineer your business processes, or sort out the processes first and then organise around them? – and partly through the personal commitment required to win over the hearts and minds at all levels.

The scale of change requires a huge, sustained effort, and the letting go by many people of things they held near and dear. Thus transformational leadership is described by Selzer and Bass[2] as: 'The process of fostering dramatic changes in an organisation by building commitment to the organisation and its mission.' Ashford and Humphrey[3] comment that 'this process is largely dependant upon the evocation, framing, and mobilisation of emotions' which the leader does by articulating a compelling, higher-order, utopian vision, and emphasising the contribution that the individual makes to the whole.

Planning

For a chief executive, the prospect of a major change programme can be terrifying. We know of one new chief executive who had been appointed by a consortium to introduce commercial management into a 300-year-old dockyard steeped in outdated managerial practices. While on holiday with his family, he could only contain his anxiety about the challenge of so much change by sitting on the beach day after day and drawing out his own detailed two-year change programme into what became a nine-feet-long critical path. This may have made him feel that things were more under control, and, as a former mega-project manager, he may have felt a lot of comfort from familiar tools, but as a means of inspiring the organisation it was a non-starter.

Mobilising the organisation

Even to start a transformation effort requires considerable bravery as well as energy. However much pressure for change there may be externally from customer demands, technology changes, or competitor moves, it is always instinctively easier for the individual to hunker down, stay where they are, and hope that the danger passes by.

So great is our inbred aversion to change that the first challenge a leader generally faces is how to get the organisation out of this state of denial and mobilised in a new direction. To do this the leader usually has to create a 'burning platform', to make it more dangerous to stay put than to move, which means he or she has to be prepared to play a highly visible role in signalling the danger, communicating the need for change and personalising the urgency.

Building the vision

One of the key ways to do this is to start to build a picture of what the upside might look like. It may at first be extremely woolly and based on intangibles, but that does not matter, since one of the tasks of the leadership group is to evolve the vision statement over time. The challenge facing the change leader is to get a critical mass of those in power to be prepared to embark on this voyage of discovery.

Personal risk

Picture the scenario. The second largest petrochemical complex in the southern hemisphere was facing closure following the withdrawal of subsidies in the wake of the political changes in South Africa. The Afrikaner managing director addressed 'town meetings' around the plant for public questioning with no questions barred on the change programme, which would undoubtedly involve some downsizing in an area where no alternative employment existed. Maybe not unusual in some other countries, but many of the black process workers had never before been given an opportunity to meet him, let alone to address him by his first name, and least of all to ask him questions. The impact his unprecedented openness made on them was significant, but for him it was major personal challenge and an emotionally draining experience to thereby make himself accountable to them, to listen to their concerns and to undertake to investigate issues they raised.

Or the leader may have to take some personal risks, to go out on a limb, in order to set an example for others to follow. For example, a point of breakthrough in a UK refinery transformation project came when Terry, the refinery manager, the ultimate representative of authority on the site, stood up in front of all his staff. They had been resisting change, because from industry surveys they already knew that they were running the third most efficient refinery in the country, and they thought that this would be enough to secure their future, despite the fact that worldwide refinery margins were plummeting.

But Terry stood up in front of them and said: 'I've been wrong in the way I've run this refinery in the past. I've realised that I need to change, and I have changed. I'm now a new man.' It was an extremely difficult admission for him to make publicly, but it had a critical impact.

When it became clear that Terry was prepared to put some of his own skin in the game, they began to take notice. As the refinery workers began to see that he did behave differently, that he listened more and became more consultative in his decision-making, they in turn began to open their minds to the possibility that they too could do things differently. After a lot of hard work, the result was a 20 per cent increase in performance, through a combination of higher-value output and lowered costs.

Sending the right signals

While a transformation effort is running, the leader also has to do a number of things that require determination and resilience. Often they will be called upon to maintain confidence levels, although they themselves may feel anything but confident that things are on track.

An organisation is highly sensitive to even the smallest unintended signal from its leader. Thus Sir John Harvey-Jones says of being chairman of ICI:[4]

One of the unexpected problems I have found in being chairman... is the fact that so many people judged the position of the company by one's own apparent mood, even to whether one smiles or not.

Holding course

The reality may well be that, after the initial excitement that accompanies the start of the new initiative, the warm fuzziness evaporates and exactly *how* you are going to make that stretch goal you committed to is revealed as decidedly unclear. After the first couple of months the first milestone slips a bit, and, after a couple more months, the benefits case starts to show holes. The leader, however, has to suppress that feeling of panic.

Making the tough calls

The leader has to make the tough calls when they are needed. These are often about people. A typical example is what to do with those who continue to resist change, usually covertly. Although one client we worked with, a Texas oilman often with a wad of chewing tobacco in his cheek, was more than ready for this challenge. 'I'll fire his ass,' he said of a senior manager who was being unsupportive of a proposed reorganisation. 'But head office is planning to transfer him to the Nigeria affiliate,' he was told. 'That's better than firing his ass,' he replied.

Often the hardest decisions concern people close to the leader – particularly colleagues who have become close friends, since there is nothing as bonding as shared experience.

Asserting themselves

Perhaps surprisingly, for some leaders the hardest thing is to assert themselves in face-to-face confrontations with colleagues, even when they are hierarchically superior. We have experienced one large organisation of national standing where for years the IT director literally terrorised, not only his peer group, but also his managing director and chairman, through his dysfunctional behaviour. Yet nothing was done until a new chairman was appointed who would stand up to him, and he was summarily removed.

Handling anxiety

One thing the leader has to contend with is the constant pressure of ambiguity and anxiety. Whether he or she is making huge investment decisions based on incomplete data, betting on the success of someone they've chosen for a key role, or supervising functions they don't understand, they have to be able to live comfortably with the risk of not being certain.

Coping with overload

There is also the problem of being overwhelmed by the sheer volume of it all, since the higher you rise, the more certain it is that, whatever your energy level (and for a leader it needs to be high), it is impossible to get done everything that needs to be done. Even if you are on top of the job, given the culture of most organisations it is easier to progress by 'workaholic', that is, compulsive, behaviour than by adhering to an unstressed lifestyle. Feeling 'OK' when leaving something undone is often hard to do.

Few leaders are known for setting themselves relaxed lifestyle standards – Gerry Robinson of Granada is reportedly one. Is it a coincidence that Sir Richard Branson, the businessman many people would now most like to identify with, projects a laid-back, more human lifestyle – wearing sweaters instead of a suit, sporting a beard, and, at one time, having a houseboat for an office?

The leadership contribution summarised

As has been outlined above, leaders have a tremendous impact on change. They can encapsulate and articulate the reasons for change, that is, they can prepare the organisation to step off the edge of a precipice by defining the future, and shaping the emerging vision. They have a critical importance in defining the new culture and role modelling how it needs to be different.

Change is almost by definition ambiguous, and transformational journeys are inevitably voyages of discovery. The leader must guide and navigate an organisation through uncharted waters. In such circumstances, leadership requires ability, courage and insight. Often it requires a leader to do something different personally, and therefore the ability and commitment to change oneself can be a critical success factor in moving an organisation towards a new future.

There are many, often varying, descriptions of leaders, some of which we have covered in the section in leadership. However, within these, there are a number of common characteristics, which are demanded in spades if a leader is to successfully deliver change. These characteristics include self-confidence, emotional stability, openness to experience it, willingness to be changed by it, and energy. While a strong intellect and technical ability are necessary to deliver change, many of the demands are to do with character and 'human strength'.

5 The Emotionally Intelligent Leader

As we have seen, the original competency sets for leaders were entirely rational but, with the recognition of charismatic or transformational leadership, new models of leadership competencies began to be developed which added an emotional component to the traditional cognitive capabilities.

In addition, the intense interest in what makes a successful leader has attracted new sorts of researchers and observers. A field that had been the preserve of the organisational psychologists has now become the stalking ground of such rare beasts as the psychoanalyst, the evolutionary psychologist and the anthropologist.

The contention now is that, far from emotional competence being an extra item on the list of capabilities, it is actually far more important for leaders in business than any other kind of competence.

One of the most popular proponents of the new emotional literacy is Daniel Goleman. In *Working with Emotional Intelligence*, he cites a global study by Hay/McBer of 15 companies, including IBM, PepsiCola and Volvo, which demonstrated that:

> Emotional competence made the crucial difference between mediocre leaders and the best. The stars showed significantly greater strengths in a range of emotional competencies, among them influence, team leadership, political awareness, self-confidence, and achievement drive. On average close to 90 per cent of their success in leadership was attributable to emotional intelligence.[1]

For Bass, the transformational leader is essentially charismatic and inspirational:

> Such leaders are able to rouse people through the sheer power of their own enthusiasm. Such leaders don't order or direct; they inspire. In articulating their vision, they are intellectually and emotionally stimulating. They show a strong belief in that vision, and they excite others

about pursuing it with them. And they are committed to nurturing relationships with those they lead.[2]

These abilities are founded on the leader's own self-awareness. Thus the
successful leader has two main capabilities: to be able to connect with,
control and leverage his or her own emotions; and to be able to do the
same with the large network of people he or she comes into contact with.
The more successful you are at the first, the easier the second becomes.

With the involvement of leadership observers of a clinical background,
our understanding of the potential impact on an organisation of the non-
cognitive becomes immensely sharper. Thus Kets de Vries talks of the
critical nature of a leader's 'inner theatre'[3] and of the destructive impact
this will have on an organisation if it is unhealthy.

He also discusses the key role a leader plays in ensuring the mental
health of their organisation. For him, every leader is 'to some extent a
kind of psychiatric social worker'.[4] This may sound extreme, but what it
means is that a leader needs to be sensitive to, contain and work with, the
emotions of their subordinates. A far cry from the problem-solving scientific manager.

Part II

Part II

Methodology

The methodology adopted for this work was based on two simultaneous approaches. First, in order to understand the business context in which the transformation occurred, existing material, including press cuttings, periodical articles and any published books, was reviewed.

Second, in order to understand the experience of transformation itself, a series of interviews was undertaken with the leader in question. The number of interviews varied from leader to leader, depending on our previous knowledge of the situation and the availability of the individual. The number of interviews typically varied from two to ten.

During the interview process, each sequence began with a general interview to lay out the tapestry of change – that is, we asked the individual to describe their background, career and the transformational journey from conception through to execution, and to signal the highlights and lowlights of the journey as they saw them. This initial interview was used as a basis to structure subsequent interviews. During these follow-up interviews, areas of the transformation were probed in more detail to further understand the events occurring at the time and, more importantly, to try to resurface and recreate the experience as the leader lived it. Where appropriate, other individuals associated with the change were later interviewed in order to gain an additional perspective on both the events and the individual. Where this has happened, it has been highlighted within a particular story.

All interviews were recorded and later transcribed. The stories told in the following sections were then put together using this material and the background data researched by authors, applying a mixture of judgement by the authors and quotations from the individuals. Once complete, the stories were shown to the individual for sign-off and approval. The individuals were each given the power of veto as to the shape and content. We have, in most cases, avoided identifying and naming other individuals involved in the change, particularly if their involvement could be perceived in any way as negative or obstructive.

In all of these stories, it is not necessarily the historical truth that matters, but rather the narrative truth, that is, the emotional experience remembered by the storyteller. In this way, this positions these stories as human experiences as opposed to business case studies.

The stories are not intended to be directly comparable; each is the story of an individual and is therefore a unique experience. Yet there are many striking differences and commonalities to be found. Conclusions drawn from the interviews are pulled together in Chapter 11.

6 Ian MacLaurin

Background of Tesco plc

Tesco plc is one of the most celebrated companies in the UK, a star of the retailing sector. Its story and successful transformation has been well documented over the years: in numerous articles, a number of books (notably *Counter Revolution – The Tesco Story*, Grafton Books, 1991, and *Tiger by the Tail*, Macmillan, 1999) and not least, in several recent TV documentaries.

Its journey from its modest origins, established by Jack Cohen operating as a street-market barrow-trader financed by his war pension, and its subsequent growth, both organically and via a number of high-profile acquisitions, its early positioning as a 'Pile It High, Sell It Cheap' supermarket chain, public ownership, expansion through Home 'n' Wear, the involvement with Green Shield stamps, to today's massive food retailing empire is a unique story.

In parallel to the business growth, there has been the intriguing story of a family business moving away from the tight control of the founding father, eventually away from the family altogether and finally into a new era of professional management. This has been accompanied by huge cultural changes, both in the retailing philosophy and in the boardroom. All of this has impacted hugely on the approach to and impact for all stakeholders; customers, employees and shareholders alike.

The statistics of the business success are well known, but a couple are worth noting here – of the 169,500 UK employees, 83,631 are shareholders and a number have become millionaires as a result of the success of the business. The company has not seen a drop in profits since 1979.

Today Tesco remains significantly ahead of its competitors in performance terms, in a range of innovations from supply chain management through employee involvement to customer focus via product introductions and rapidly expanding product range, as well as in cultural terms. Tesco's transformation has been far-reaching and conclusive, moving itself away from its 'Pile It High, Sell It Cheap' origins to becoming a quality operator with professional management (data driven, customer oriented) and strong teamwork across a cohesive and growing business. Much of this change has been catalysed and driven by Ian MacLaurin who joined

31

the business in 1959 as a management trainee. Today Tesco is poised to enter the overseas arena via involvement in the Far East and is positioned for ongoing and growing success within the UK retail market.

Ian MacLaurin

Ian MacLaurin, 62, is the consummate professional. On a first meeting he comes across as somewhat diffident, quiet and thoughtful but quickly puts one at ease with his charming manner. He is charismatic in a calm and controlled way. His office just around the corner from the Houses of Parliament is comfortable and workmanlike, with the books and artefacts reflecting his passions in life; his family, golf and cricket. He is disarmingly open and honest and tells the Tesco story with clarity and passion. The consistency with which he recounts the story of Tesco is impressive; there is little difference in either emphasis or content in how he has retold it across the years for a number of different articles or forums – this is characteristic of his typical evenness and control of his emotions. He has obviously spent a significant amount of time going over the critical events of his career in his mind, thinking carefully about the key issues and events. In doing this he has undoubtedly processed some of the raw emotion that surrounded the dramatic twists and turns of the Tesco transformation and tells the story with care and logic, and in such a way as to protect the feelings of those involved, and to play down his own role in the events. This is entirely consistent with the impression he conveys of being considered, rational and analytical, yet well able to recall events from a number of years ago with passion and a recollection of the emotional impact it had on him and the others involved. Yet his human warmth and ability to empathise are obvious to see and have undoubtedly been the key factors in his huge success in what is fundamentally a people business.

Background and career path

Born in 1937, he is the only child of a loving and gentle family. His father was a senior civil servant, and both parents were extremely nurturing and supportive. Neither placed excessive expectations on him as a child but respected him for the individual he was. His mother would have liked him to be a teacher or similar professional and confessed to being somewhat disappointed when he went into retail. His father was sports mad and was delighted to have a son who had similar interests and not insignificant skills in this area.

Ian was educated at Malvern College, which was a 'very happy time' for him. He distinguished himself particularly on the sports field and most particularly in cricket. It was in the sports arena that he got his first, early taste of responsibility as captain of a number of sports teams. This responsibility he relished and took extremely seriously. The early leadership skills he learnt here around identifying and playing to individual strengths and exploiting these stood him in great stead throughout his career. It was also in the sports arena that a number of his key characteristics were shaped. The early lessons he learnt stayed with him throughout his professional career. A couple of his sports masters were key mentors. He cites two examples in particular that had a huge and lasting impact on him. First, he describes how, having made the cricket side as a youngster, he was sitting waiting to bat. His sports master, waiting with him, asked him what he considered to be a good score. The young Ian thought and responded 'I reckon 20 to 30 is a pretty good score for me'. His sports master turned to him and said 'you're a batsman, you've failed unless you score a hundred!' Ian goes on to say, 'and I suppose I've thought about that many times in my life and the message came through to me that if you've got any sort of ability at all, then maximise it, don't go for second best. Don't go for 30 when you should go for the hundred!'

His football master was equally influential. Ian quotes a story to illustrate the point.

We were playing soccer against Oxford University and it was 0–0 with five minutes to go. We scored and the centre forward and I celebrated – shook hands, arms around the shoulder, that sort of thing – very minor stuff, particularly when you see the way they behave nowadays. The master came up to us; he was refereeing for the school, and he said, 'Stop that! You're here to score goals and I don't want either of you to continue to make an exhibition of yourselves!' The message that came through loudly and clearly to me was 'Get on with the job, you're there to do a job! Don't be flamboyant with it. Just get on and get your head down and do it!' So those two fellows, both of whom are still alive, had a big, big influence on my life.

The style these interventions encouraged has stayed with him throughout his career – there are few recorded instances of him having displayed extremes of emotion at any time – indeed his ability to maintain his equanimity was critical in allowing him to effect a shift in culture away from the old-style Tesco. In talking about this Ian says, 'Oh, sometimes I get annoyed. Not too often I hope. I don't think there is a lot of point in it really. But sometimes I do get a bit upset.'

His success on the sports field was enormous; he played cricket for Kent and would certainly have gone on to play for England and followed the career of a professional sport person. Instead, on leaving school he completed his National Service with RAF Fighter Command and worked for a short period with a firm of domestic appliance manufacturers. He continued playing cricket and while on tour in the south of England happened to meet Jack Cohen at the Grand Hotel in Eastbourne, where Cohen was spending a short holiday with his family. Ian, along with his cricket colleagues, was introduced to him and was immediately struck by Cohen's personal aura. 'He was a very charismatic character – when he spoke all other conversation stopped – everyone hung on to his every word. There was a powerful aura about him – he was a very special fellow.' The impression he made on Ian was enormous and somewhat uncharacteristically Ian resolved to meet him again, 'he spurred me on to do something,' and a few days later followed up the introduction with a phone call arranging to meet Cohen in his office. Ian went to this meeting without any clear intent or plan as to what might happen, 'I just knew there was something I wished to pursue'. He came out of the meeting with a job offer and joined Tesco in 1959 as its first management trainee.

On joining Tesco, he quickly discovered that management training, or indeed training of any kind, was pretty much non-existent. Like all other new joiners, Ian was thrown in at the deep end, reliant on his own resources and learning the business of retail from the grassroots up. He loved it; particularly he loved the contact with people, both his colleagues and the customers.

> My sporting background had given me a grounding in people skills, and I loved getting out there. I found it very easy to relate to people, and I was there at a time when they were starting to open up – they were happy to tell me what they thought about the business and what needed to change. It was an eye-opening experience.

His early business style was, not surprisingly, similar to the style he had employed so successfully as sports captain at school. It was focused on people as individuals, understanding their motivations, identifying their strengths and playing to these. He also learned to listen carefully to the requirements of customers, and as his knowledge of the business grew he increasingly used this data to support his own growing intuition as to what would and would not work in the increasingly competitive retail arena. His conclusions were derived from careful analysis. His teams, even at this early stage, were characterised by great spirit and commercial success and, as his confidence, knowledge and reputation grew, he rapidly worked his way up through the management ranks. He was able to get the best out of people; he was a great team player, yet always the captain.

By the end of the 1960s, he had become regional managing director – south. Tesco, as a whole, was beginning to struggle in an increasingly price competitive world and Ian's success in the south contrasted sharply with the fortunes of the northern business. In 1970 he was asked to take over this operation, replacing at short notice the incumbent managing director. This was typical of the style of management common at the time. The business was not operated as a team:

> It was a group of people who were very jealous of each other, if they could skewer each other they would have done so. People were continually jockeying for position. Jack positively encouraged this culture – it was entirely in line with his style of management. He believed that such conflicts strengthened his own position and actively encouraged them. This was fundamentally different to my belief that as leader you are captain of the team and your role is to get everyone rowing together.

Once again he enjoyed huge success and in 1971 he was appointed to the board.

Divide and rule – the style in the boardroom

By now Tesco was going through a period of great difficulty, struggling to maintain market share, under pressure from the City and handicapped by conflict in the boardroom. The business was nominally under the chairmanship of Hyman Kreitman but Jack Cohen still very much called the shots. Cohen was an entrepreneur and consummate trader and had built his empire on these qualities. He believed 'a feel for the market and a good head for figures was what business was all about'. He had never pursued a planned policy – indeed he would have scorned such a notion – and still preferred to go with his own instinct, encouraging others throughout the business to do likewise.

Jack Cohen was a follower of the divide and rule doctrine. His style in the boardroom was domineering and somewhat brutal – he was given to outbursts and personal attacks:

There were the most terrible up-and-downers. He wouldn't speak to anybody, banged doors, all that stuff; although he rarely bore a grudge for long, believing 'tomorrow is another day'.

My wife probably summed up the board atmosphere best. We used to meet them socially and she once said to me 'I couldn't stand all this, all this bickering and unpleasantness', but although it was very traumatic, I used to largely let it go over my head and then I'd go out and do exactly what I wanted to do, what I believed was right. At the end of the day, it was the numbers that counted and if I produced decent figures then everyone was happy and everyone would forget about all the squabbles! So I listened to the emotion flying around and just got on with it.

It had been clear for some time that the board was not working effectively, the remit of discussions was too broad and unfocused and failed consistently to attempt to address any of the really critical issues of the day. Voting was the order of the day, and Cohen invariably won; he was not averse to applying personal pressure to sway board members to his point of view. It was into this arena, characterised in *Counter Revolution* as a 'snake-pit' that Ian arrived as a new board member: 'everyone was jealous of each other, and trying to out-manoeuvre each other – they were like politicians trying to massage their own egos.' It was a key period of learning. Ian admired Cohen for his talent as a trader and retailer, for the commitment and passion he had applied in building the business, but through his own experience, and through his own application of the 'retail is detail' maxim, he knew that if the business were to survive and prosper something different had to be done. 'Jack was dominant in the business he had founded, but as things changed he had failed to update his vision. At this time he should have gone – it would have been better for the business. By staying around and trying to maintain control he almost destroyed the business he had created.'

The future had to be different to the past; intuition had to be supplemented with data that must be decisively and consistently acted upon. Ian's own style of management and leadership was diametrically opposed to that of Cohen, and Ian was not afraid to take on anyone or anything in doing the right thing for the business. Cohen led with his emotions and latterly had used them as a tool and a weapon, effectively to create a culture of fear and, to a large extent, immobility. Ian, while clearly subject to the same pressures and frustrations, was able, as a result of his contrasting background and personality, to internalise and manage his emotions. He was thus able to present a powerful contrast to the prevailing culture, a contrast that effectively became the lightening rod for change.

Everything from management style to emotional reaction was different between Ian and Cohen. This contrast implicitly threw in to focus the forthcoming battle – that between the old and the new, the intuitive and the rational, the market-trader and the professional, the individual and the team, the short term and the long term, the past and the future. The battle-lines were drawn early; leadership through personality and the ability to overcome personal ego – a battle of almost fairytale dimensions. The ability to use emotional make-up in the most effective way was to be a key component in leading the transformation of Tesco.

Fortunately Ian was not alone in the realisation that things needed to change radically. There was an emerging breed of retailers within the business, mentored under the guidance of Arthur Thrush, who saw the need for change. The boardroom thus faced a growing challenge; a face-off existed between the beliefs of the old guard and the convictions of the new.

As the business entered the 1970s, the conflict continued and, to the consternation of the City, the business appeared to lose its way – Tesco was beginning to lose its price competitiveness and failing to deliver on its key promise to consumers. Gone were the days of 'Pile It High, Sell It Cheap', but nothing had yet emerged to replace it. The conflict as to where the future lay was strengthening. Trading suffered and, in order to maintain appearances, results were increasingly demanded by head office; prices went up in an attempt to deliver against these pressures, and Tesco continued to erode its price competitiveness. A vicious circle set in. In 1974, Leslie Porter took over as chairman after Hyman Kreitman resigned, having found life under his father-in-law 'intolerable'. Leslie Porter initially split the management function between two new MDs, Laurie Leigh for non-foods and Ian MacLaurin for retailing and foodstuffs. That year saw an almost 20 per cent drop in profits. For Ian, it was the period of major frustration:

> it was clear something fundamental needed to be done yet I couldn't influence what was happening. Jack was unwell, getting older and losing any vision of the future. Yet he would not relinquish control, and was increasingly jealous of anyone other than his own name being used in the press, 'I am the chairman of this company, I am the president', it was very difficult to signal publicly any kind of change or have an impact on the future.

As time went on, Ian emerged as the leader of the new guard, arguing for root and branch change and increasingly he took on the mantle for leading the drive for change against the old guard, led by Jack Cohen, who continued to defend the principles upon which Tesco had been founded. Ian was not shackled to the past and believed there were no sacred cows in defining the needs of the future.

The business continued, still running as it was on feudal lines as a result of the divide and rule doctrine, finding it almost impossible to stick to a strategy, the old entrepreneurial activity being still in primacy. The stores effectively ran their own price lists, making it very difficult to gain control of the key levers of the business. This made nonsense of logical marketing and logical accounting. The whole business required a radical restructuring. Ian emerged as the key driver for focusing the need for change and led the revolution away from gut feeling to professional management.

In addition to its internal problems, Tesco had a number of significant problems in the marketplace, which were hampering its room for manoeuvre – Tesco was not considered by many as the retailer of choice. As a result, when planning new developments, a local authority would be most likely to approach Sainsbury's and/or Marks & Spencer. Tesco would be unlikely to be considered, having acquired a reputation as 'something of a retail cowboy'. This situation had huge risks, primarily because it could ultimately result in Tesco being trapped in small, increasingly unsuitable and inadequate retail sites, thereby finding it almost impossible to break out into a new way of retailing. Ian knew this had to change, and realised that in order to do so he needed to change the hearts and minds of the planners who took key decisions around which retailers to work with. In 1975, Ian delivered the first of the company's Occasional Papers in a bid to re-establish Tesco's development credentials. He basically argued that planners and retailers needed each other and needed to work together to deliver to the shopping public what would best serve their interests. He argued for the need for full consultation and agreement. This fundamentally changed the relationship between Tesco and local authorities and laid the platform for Tesco's hugely successful development programme over the next few years. This was an important step in positioning Tesco to change its image and break away from the physical shackles of its history. Culturally, it was a significant step in changing the management philosophy and practice of the organisation, signalling a move towards a new rational approach.

In 1976, he surprised market observers with a speech, 'The Management Factor', to an audience of brokers. The speech was analytical, data driven and thoughtful. It was astonishing to hear it from Tesco. Suddenly Tesco, with Ian MacLaurin at the forefront, began to emerge as a very different organisation. This clearly established Ian, and by association Tesco, as a different kind of retailer. Yet, despite beginning the process of changing people's perception of Tesco, in reality the business still clung doggedly to its old style of razzmatazz and Day-Glo visual heritage. Green Shield stamps continued to be Tesco's prime, and arguably only, tool in marketing competitiveness.

Green Shield stamps

Green Shield stamps were a trading stamp, a concept first introduced in the USA. The stamps were given as a reward against purchases made in a particular retailer. The stamps could then be pasted in a book and saved for later redemption against other merchandise (it would, for example, be theoretically possible to save for such items as a television or other similar luxury items) or, more rarely, cash (albeit that the face value of the stamps was minimal). When prices, products and services are similar, a customer will award patronage impartially as long as there is no ongoing benefit to be gained from systematic attachment to a particular retailer. Trading stamps were effectively a form of deferred discount. When first introduced, the stamps tended to reinforce customer loyalty at a time of intensifying competition in the high street.

Trading stamps were administered by independent businesses that supplied retailers with stamps, stamp books, catalogues and all the other necessary merchandise for when customers handed in their books for redemption. In return the retailer was charged a percentage of sales – typically about 2 per cent of turnover. The Green Shield Company was established in 1958 and, amidst much controversy in the retail market, signed a deal with Tesco in 1963. This was controversial with, and opposed by, suppliers and competing retailers. The Green Shield/Tesco partnership was instrumental in transforming the shopping habits and expectations of the British shopper, and played a crucial part in Tesco's growth in the 1960s, reinforcing its reputation at the time as providing value to the consumer.

Facing the future

Many of the new guard instinctively, and through reasoned, local research, doubted the ongoing value of the stamps and believed that a broader approach to competitiveness was necessary. This was a subject of fierce contention within the boardroom. Some localised test marketing, heavily opposed by Jack Cohen, indicated that the new guard was indeed correct on this point. By early 1976, there was a growing conviction that a break with Green Shield stamps was inevitable and Ian, as the leader of the new guard, was instructed to find a new agency to relaunch Tesco. Both the power and the future philosophy within the boardroom were beginning to make fundamental shifts.

Later that year, under the direction of the board, Ian commissioned the agency McCann Erickson to undertake a major piece of research to understand the consumer view and what was really happening in the marketplace. This research had two key findings: on price, Tesco's image was better than the reality, and on quality, the reality was better than the image. These findings sent shock waves through the board. Fundamental change was inevitable. The future had to look different to the past if the business were to survive. A strategy had to be found to move the business forward. 'This was make or break time for me. Of course I was scared, but I knew the research was pointing us in the right direction, and I also knew we had a lot to overcome and we needed time from the City to effect the future.'

Breaking with the past – the turning point

In early 1977, the board met to consider 'the most important decision the company would ever have to make regarding its trading philosophy – whether or not to break with Green Shield stamps.' Jack Cohen argued vociferously for continuing with what had helped shape the success of the past, and Ian MacLaurin led the challenge for a different future. Reflecting back he says:

> I spent a lot of time in the field, round the stores, I was closer to the customers than anybody else on the board. And I could see that the customers just didn't want stamps and I could see what our competitors were doing. Asda were starting up successfully in the north, Sainsbury's were powering away without stamps and doing very well in the middle to upper market, and there was Tesco really struggling at the bottom end of the market. I knew that we had to change. My people working with me also knew we had to change, but the real challenge was swinging the board around to believing that we had to reposition the business and change and drop stamps. From a personal point of view I had been in the company since 1959, so I'd been there nearly 20 years and worked desperately hard in that time, working my way up to the main board, to be managing director, and I didn't want to see all that thrown away. I

wanted to see the business go forward and really had no choice but to try and persuade the founding fathers, who had made the decision to go into stamps, and who weren't now going round the stores, and who were settled into their own lifestyles, to change. In many ways, it was really just good common sense, but of course at the time it wasn't, it was highly emotional. Furthermore, I was one of only, I think, two people on the board who weren't Jewish, and I wasn't one of, nor related to, the founding fathers.

The situation was highly emotional. The stakes and the tension were high. 'I knew I had the power of the shops and the shop executives behind me, but the board meeting was very traumatic' and, in the tradition of the day, the decision went to a vote. The result was 5–5. Describing the day, Ian recalls:

Jack Cohen turned to Leslie Porter and said 'Leslie, you're the chairman, you have the casting vote' but I said, 'Hold on, I have a letter from David Behar that supports my side, …David wants to come out. So, Mr Chairman, we've won, we've won 6–5.'

That was quite a tense moment, shall we say. The old man couldn't believe it! He'd never, the family had never, lost a vote in the history of the company, they'd never lost a vote ever!

Jack Cohen, who was in his seventies then and not well, demanded that the vote be taken again. It was – the result stood at 6–5. In all, the vote was taken five or six times during the course of that board meeting and the result remained 6–5 throughout. 'I think he was hoping against hope that one of my side would, I suppose, be fearful of him and change their mind, but no one moved and the result stood!'

The way Ian describes this critical moment is typically understated. He recollects the fear of losing, the competitiveness of the result, his frustration at the battles he'd had in getting to that moment (he almost quit at one point) and the anxiety of the day itself. Yet he was able to subsume these to the pursuit of the future – his aspiration and drive for the business of the future were more important to him than seeking personal position. His focus was on winning the war, not just the battle in hand.

The result of the board meeting had far-reaching consequences. Not only did it clear the way for a relaunch of the business and a move towards a new future; it also effectively brought Cohen's reign to an end.

After the meeting he came into my office and he got hold of the lapels of my jacket and shook me, he really shook me. He was furious. He said, 'if this fails, you know what is going to happen to you?' I took his hands away and said, 'I'm absolutely certain what's going to happen to me if it fails. But, Sir John, I don't think it will.' And so, as we moved towards the Jubilee weekend in June, we began to get the show on the road.

The impact of the emotion had another key effect on Ian. 'A big, big lesson came to me, through all that. I swore I would never stay on in the company too long. Jack Cohen founded the company, he was a brilliant entrepreneurial retailer, but in the end he almost bankrupted the business he founded.' This lesson later led Ian to introduce a policy for compulsory retirement at 60.

'Check-out'

'Check-out' was the marketing campaign to be put in to replace Green Shield stamps. The drive for its design and introduction consumed huge passion and energy for everyone throughout the business over the coming weeks. 'Morale is the lifeblood of retailing and "Check-out" was aimed as much at our own people as at our customers. Our future depended on its success – we needed to generate new life within the business.' The relaunch was advertised for 8 June and at the start of the previous weekend all the shops were closed down, all the windows were whitewashed and advertisements about the reopening were placed. Although Tesco was not given a huge chance of success by industry advisers, there was massive interest from customers and rival retailers to see what was going on. During this time, the team completely remerchandised the stores, repriced everything, put new tickets up everywhere so that the business would present a completely new image to the customer when it reopened.

We knew our prices were very aggressive indeed, we were going back to the old Tesco of aggressive price cutting. When we had everything on stream, we did not open on the Wednesday as trailed. Instead we went a day later; we planned this to take the competitors off balance. Instead, on that Wednesday, the national press was full of rivals' adverts exhorting customers to shop with them, advertising their new prices. As planned, we had booked space for the Thursday morning and advertised our prices that were even better value. Fantastic value. We cleaned the windows down in preparation for reopening.

This was a really tense time. We'd worked so hard at getting to this point and now all the work we had done was on the line. We were tired and emotional, we'd had very little sleep for several days and we were absolutely exhausted. Our future and that of thousands of others was on the line – it was a very scary moment.

On that Wednesday evening I met in my office with David Malpas. We had a large Scotch and I remember saying, 'Well, this time tomorrow we will know if we've still got a job.' We staggered off home and I woke up on that Thursday morning and spent the day going around the stores – it was a phenomenal success. The business simply took off. It was just amazing! Phone calls were coming in from all over the country. At that time we had nearly 900 stores of all shapes and sizes and it was a huge success. We were up and running.

Competitors, market observers, and even some of Tesco's own staff thought that the success would be short lived. Turnover was soon up by 30 per cent, volume by 43 per cent and very quickly the continuing success started to put huge stresses and strains on the business. It began to be extremely difficult to service the stores: 'The stores were struggling to stay open – how we kept going at all was a tribute to our people.' Tesco was threatening to kill itself through its own success. Weaknesses were exposed in most of the major operational areas. Systems were still largely primitive and the management structure was far from being modern. Ian and his team sat down and looked at the future and knew that it could not work without a radical restructuring right across the business. 'It was very clear we had to reposition, we needed to close down stores we could not manage. We needed a top-to-tail refurbishment of the company and all its systems.'

The break with the past would be dramatic and far-reaching. There were few systematic policies and procedures across the business, up until now stores had largely operated separately, managers had pretty much looked after themselves, stocking pretty much what they wanted to. The regions had effectively been four separate armies. There was no cohesive approach to the marketplace. Internally things were as bad, co-ordinated buying was a rarity, rather entrepreneurial activity and individual enterprise still ruled. A measured strategic approach was almost entirely lacking from the business.

Throughout this time pressure on the business continued. The City, watching closely from the sidelines, did not give Tesco a price at all. Tesco's claim that 'we are going to do a Sainsbury's and Tesco quality is going to be as good as Marks & Spencer's was met with incredulity.

Something had to be done quickly. In order to harness and build on the success of 'Check-out' centralisation had to be a key strategic priority. Private enterprise was out, centralised buying in, with all that implied for suppliers and for line management. A controlled range had to be put in place. Centralisation inevitably led to a loss of power for line managers. The priority was to provide these managers with service. 'Check-out' re-affirmed the maxim that 'retail is detail'; it caused a rethink across the entire business and taught Tesco the need for teamwork and the importance of professionalism. All of these changes led inevitably to a revolution in the information technology that supported the business. The new strategy also required Tesco to step up to another urgent issue, namely how to sell the new image out of inadequate and ageing stores. This hastened progress in the development of out-of-town hypermarkets. The business was rapidly moving away from short-termism towards long-term planning. Tesco developed a burgeoning reputation as the thinking retailer. As Ian MacLaurin was later to say when describing this period:

> The improvement of intuition is a highly technical matter.

> I believe retailers are born, not made – I think I was born to be a retailer. Retailers have to have a very clear intuition about what has to happen. What we had to do after 'Check-Out', and what others in the business had failed to do, was to put the 'technical' piece on top of this intuition to make it truly effective. You were dead unless you could make this happen. We knew what we wanted – our intuition was good, but the implementation of this was critical – this was the difficult bit!

Transformation and the journey to maturity

Over the next decade the company was to undergo a fundamental change in its attitude towards itself. It successfully managed to transform itself across a number of key dimensions moving out of inadequate and tiny outlets and becoming a quality retailer operating out of modern super-stores; gone was the family culture where all the real power lay with family members; in its place there was a cohesive and modern business, underpinned by teamwork and professional management.

> We had built a very good team of people. You want people that have the ambition to achieve and to share in your vision, but you want them to

come from a different viewpoint. They each brought a different perspective to the business and collectively it was a very strong team, probably one of the strongest retail teams there has ever been, otherwise we wouldn't have been so successful. I led the team, but the team worked together; it was the most wonderful team to work with and very exciting. And then of course you get success and it all starts to go; all sorts of other things start fitting into place after that and it begins to take off.

Ian's enjoyment of people and his skill in getting them to work together as a team is clear when he talks about this period.

Step by step, under Ian's guidance, Tesco continued to professionalise both its operation and its image. It is hard to find a parallel to the phenomenal success of the rebirth of Tesco in 1977. In the minds of many people its acquisition of the Hillards chain in 1987 confirmed its transformation and new maturity. Observers to this acquisition, which was undertaken with textbook precision, described it as 'a lesson in takeover tactics'. By the mid-1980s the business was producing impressive results – indeed the business has not seen a profit downturn since 1979.

In 1985 Ian MacLaurin took over the chairmanship of the company. Under his chairmanship the boardroom style changed significantly; the board never again took a vote on any issue but reached agreement via reasoned debate – a significant and crucial contrast to the past.

We had a very, very cohesive board, including some excellent non-executives, all of whom had bought into the ambition for the future. They were, however, by no means a tame board and we had some highly animated discussions and a number of significant disagreements. However, the process was very democratic and at the end of the day we all bought in to the final decision and supported it moving forward.

When asked about his reputed 'black look', Ian laughs and says, 'yes, I suppose the chairman did from time to time have a black look; he did not always get his way you know, but that is all it was – a black look.'

The 1980s were a time of growth in profits, reputation, market share and overall standing. In short, it was a huge success story. In time, the success led to a degree of arrogance and, when the business went into the recession of the early 1990s, it hit a small, but not serious hiccup. 'We didn't anticipate the economic slowdown as we probably should have done, but we soon realised it and got the business back on track.' Overcoming this arrogance was another time of frustration for Ian:

We got arrogant at this point. The market changed and started to move against us. For a while we thought we knew better than the marketplace we were trying to serve, the Sainsbury's syndrome, and ignored it. We stopped listening to what the market was telling us and, as a consequence, were slow to react. As a result, we had a dodgy few months, but we quickly readjusted and learned the lesson. I learned the lesson. I was in charge and should have seen it earlier. Don't get arrogant, and we never did again.

Having reset the direction of the business, he was able to concentrate on identifying and nurturing the talent for the future. He stuck to his commitment of retiring at 60 and left the business in 1997.

Having laid down rules and regulations that we would retire at 60 regardless of position, the other great thing I think we did was to identify and groom our succession. Those guys have now been in charge for over two years, and Tesco has gone from strength to strength. That's brilliant. You know, for me to sit here and see Tesco consolidating its position and going to Thailand and developing, that is tremendous. It's tremendous.

This ongoing legacy clearly gives him great personal satisfaction.

And so the transition was complete; from market street-trader through 'Pile It High, Sell It Cheap' to quality operator in prime sites. It is a story of contrasting styles and values, of how one business made a journey from entrepreneurial start-up to professional management, of how the shift was made from 'where once it was a case of all against the rest, today Tesco is a team'. Ian MacLaurin, who was knighted in 1989 for services to the industry, crafted and piloted the journey, through a strong belief in leadership, playing to people's strengths and being the best that he could be. In a uniquely people business, he felt sufficiently strongly about what he was doing to enable a rational approach to overcome a highly emotional and ill-disciplined legacy. By not being shackled to the past and afraid to take risks, through his belief in analysis to take on anybody or anything, he demonstrated that thought-leadership and captaincy could achieve the extraordinary. A warm and passionate leader, he was able to manage his own emotional needs and reactions to deliver for the team he led. This he was able to do through a deep self-confidence and belief in doing the right thing. He recognises that in doing this, he often paid a price in terms of the amount of time he was able to spend with his family.

On retiring from Tesco, he has refocused his life around his family and his continuing passion in the sports field. He took over as chairman of the

England and Wales Cricket board, an experience he has found both frustrating and enlightening. In addition, he is now chairman of Vodafone, the largest capitalised company in the UK. Both of these experiences he talks about in his memoir *Tiger by the Tail* (Macmillan, 1999).

Reflections

Having spent time in going over the Tesco story, we spent a little time talking about a few of the things that seemed important background. The impression was strongly reinforced that Ian is focused very much on the team, rather than the individual, that he is perceptive around what drives people, and, despite his achievements, is modest and analytical around what has driven them. His confidence and calm were clearly crucial in the extraordinary journey.

Who do you most admire in business and why?

I admire John Sainsbury in our business, the retail business. He's very good, he loved the business, he knew the business, he was very autocratic, not a team player, but he drove the business forward. If you look at his time as chairman of Sainsbury's, it was the most successful time they ever had. Quite interesting, because his problem was when he left, he was so autocratic that he left no team. David Sainsbury took over; he was a team player but had no team to play with. So the Sainsbury business started to go downhill. I think John is a bit to blame for that.

On responsibility and retirement

Opportunities for responsibility are always there if you take them seriously. When you are given responsibility, some people take it, some people can cope with it, some people thrive on it, other people can't stand it, can't cope with it, don't thrive on it. But I like responsibility. I really enjoy it. I love thrusting forward. I love to see a business progress.

The lesson, the more you look at it, is that you can be responsible for a business over a period of time and then you should move on (10 to 12 years in the hot seat is, I think, the absolute maximum), then you should go and do something else. There are lots of examples to support this.

Let's face it, if you are the CEO or chairman of a company, it is a very nice existence – it's hugely responsible because you asked to be responsible for the way the business goes, your lifestyle, and the people around you who are there to help. In Tesco I just had to pick up the phone and things happened. You get used to that but you must never take it for granted.

I determined early on that I would not stay for too long – I had seen what happens in that case! It is your responsibility and duty to identify the next generation and to move on.

On his style versus Jack Cohen's style

We were absolutely diametrically opposite. Jack Cohen came up through the East End of London. He was born in the East End in the early part of the century, went through the First World War, came out and, as did a lot of Jewish people, fought for his very existence. As a young lad, he had so much to contend with it was untrue, but he was very successful, although he had to fight like cat and dog to get it. These difficulties showed throughout his career in his style. As a manager, he set people against each other all the time. He was absolutely rule and divide and that made things very difficult for people. He was very much on the defensive, aggressive and jealous of others' success. He used to go wild if there was anything in the press that was not under his name. Petty jealousies like this happened all the time. He made life very difficult for people; in fact he made life so intolerable for his own son-in-law that he drove him out of the business. It was traumatic. Yes, quite traumatic but pretty interesting.

Our differences were great, the upbringing I had, through public school, playing all the sport, involved in teams, appreciating people. I had to work hard to achieve what I did, but it was different for me, my very existence was never in threat and I was able to put things aside and allow reasoned debate to rule. Of course, I felt the same emotions and pressures, but they did not dominate me in quite the same way.

7   Richard Ide

Background of Volkswagen UK

Volkswagen UK has been an outstanding success story, moving from being an also-ran car importer with negligible market share to a highly profitable, prestige business with a leading market position. Today it has a market share of 10.7 per cent and a turnover of £3.2 billion. It spans five brands; the top-of-the-market Audi, increasingly rivalling the long-established brands of BMW and Mercedes; the mass-market Volkswagen which revolutionised the middle market with the hugely successful VW Golf and Polo, both of which have made quality and technical excellence a prerequisite for this segment; and Skoda, once laughed at, but which now regularly scores the highest customer satisfaction ratings of any player in the industry. Newcomer SEAT and the commercial vehicles (CV) business complete the Group.

Over the last ten years, the company has changed on almost every dimension: product, ownership, technology, staff numbers, organisation structure and culture.

While the German parent company has managed the revolution of the product under Dr Piech's common platform strategy, the UK organisation has, from a business perspective, quietly transformed itself. Today it is the most successful car importer business in the UK, a jewel in the Volkswagen empire and a leading example of a highly leveraged, lean enterprise. Its dealers, across all five brands, enjoy returns that are the envy of many of the rival marques.

The scale of the management change over this period is impressive; sales revenue has increased by 300 per cent, volume 2.5-fold, profit has substantially increased, headcount has been reduced by 60 per cent and business processes, from technology through vehicle logistics, have been successfully outsourced. Today the business is a prestige employer where the average age of the employees is 36 years.

All of these changes have been masterminded and driven from the UK headquarters, now a high-tech showcase for the product, in Milton Keynes and has been led by Richard Ide, the UK MD.

Richard Ide

Richard Ide, 61, is a tall, quietly spoken man with an easy manner and a distinguished air. He has a desk on the ground floor of the modern open-plan office, but, when in Milton Keynes, was more often than not to be found working, jacket off, with a colleague at one of the two comfortable sofas which sat to the left of his desk. Much of the work in his final months as MD was around coaching his colleagues, building and nurturing the talent for tomorrow. He greeted visitors with a welcome smile that quickly put them at their ease, however, it was not long before they became aware of the sharp intellect and natural authority which Richard brings to all his business dealings. He immediately impresses people with a sense of integrity and focus. This gravitas is a key element of Richard's success. Over the years, he has developed a style which has allowed him to leverage this without being too intimidating to those around him. Nonetheless, he has a well-earned reputation for steeliness.

Richard has a family background steeped in the motor industry, yet he is quite unlike many of the macho, so-called, 'petrol heads' so often to be found in leadership positions in many of the leading automotive organisations. Indeed, as Richard became more directly exposed to the industry, he was so appalled by what he found that he made a promise to himself to change whatever he could, so that both he and those close to him could be proud of the businesses with which they were associated. The work he has done at Milton Keynes has not only transformed the VW UK Group, but also significantly impacted on the car retailing industry. By the time the current strategy is fully implemented, he, together with his team, will have succeeded in changing forever the way in which things happen in this industry, leaving a legacy to all those who purchase new vehicles. Expected forthcoming changes in legislation are certain to have far-reaching consequences for car retailing in the UK, but it is likely that Richard's work will have positioned the UK Group for success, whatever the changing environment.

Richard retired from the business at the end of 1999, leaving behind him an organisation equipped, enthusiastic and able to continue his crusade. His personal standing both within the organisation, and more broadly in the industry, was extremely high. Although it had taken him 40 years to get himself to a position to make his dream for the motor industry a reality, his achievement at Milton Keynes will stand as testimony. This is his story.

Richard is married to Julie. They have two sons and live deep in the Oxfordshire countryside, a 45-minute commute to the office. The subsequent drive has given him the opportunity for valuable thinking and decompression time. Outside work, his passion is for hunting. He is at his happiest when out with his horses or walking in the countryside – something he has always turned to when under pressure, allowing him to clear his mind and creating the environment for him to do much of his best thinking.

Background and career path

Richard comes from a family with a strong tradition in the car industry. His father was an early apprentice at General Motors. His family was a close one, made even closer by the tragedy of losing an elder son when Richard was seven. Richard grew up effectively as an only child and as a consequence spent a significant amount of time in the company of adults. He attributes his self-confidence and self-belief to having been 'treated as a competent adult by those around me from the age of 12'. It was a highly supportive and encouraging family background, but not one where good ideas alone were enough. 'If I wanted to cycle to Rome, my parents' reaction would have been "great idea but for goodness sake don't just say it, get your bike out of the garage!"' Failure was not considered an option.

Inevitably, much of the discussion and social life in his home revolved around the motor industry and it was not surprising that he should become involved in motor sport, something he did with a characteristic degree of success, competing successfully at both the national and international level. He did not find school inspiring and left at 16 'with three O-levels and a lousy school report', to follow his father's example and start an apprenticeship at Vauxhall. By this time his father was running a car dealership. On his father's advice, and wishing to both maintain a separation between his hobby and his career and to carve his own way in life, he chose to enter the newly emerging CV business, where he would be away from the direct influence of his father.

Once in the CV business, there followed a period when he learned the business from the bottom up; out on the road 'working his heart out', finding a way to have an impact and deliver success. At the retail end, the volume truck business was in the early stages of separating from cars and the first stand-alone truck dealerships were beginning to emerge. Starting out as the most junior salesman when it took many months to sell anything at all, Richard quickly grew to love the business because of the access and insight it gave him into people and their businesses. It was an excellent training ground in business and Richard soon found a way of having an impact. His style was built on trust, getting to know the customer, what really counted for them and then delivering against this requirement to the best of his ability.

Having early on established a reputation as someone who could deliver results, Richard was headhunted through a variety of roles of increasing complexity in which he had responsibility for the entire business. In these he built and refined his business philosophy and grew his confidence in his own ability:

> it underpinned my individuality, my sense of being alone, my faith in being able to work out what was right and going for it, my willingness to trust my own instinct and my own judgement, and, not insignificantly, it gave me a huge knowledge of basic things like cashflow and accounting.

Even at this early stage in his career, he measured and prided himself on always leaving behind a better business than had been there before he joined it. During this period, he had the opportunity to supplement the skills he had acquired on the ground with formal academic training (at INSEAD and the Harvard Business School). This he found a very enlightening experience. It reaffirmed his belief in his own instincts – the things he had learnt on the ground were now supported by the weight of academic research and insight. It confirmed to him that what he was doing was right, while simultaneously challenging and offering him new frameworks for thinking about the future. He began to think about the art of the possible.

Eventually in 1982, after a series of increasingly responsible roles in the CV business, a conversation with headhunters led to an introduction with Lonrho. Lonrho at the time owned the Volkswagen Audi importer business in the UK, and in addition had just taken over the MAN commercial vehicle business. This business was not selling many trucks and was losing a lot of money. Richard was recruited with a brief to 'sort it out; close it or do something'. He met the MAN team in Munich and liked them. He agreed to join and once again found himself in a situation he relished – a challenge to turn things round and improve the business. With the role, came a seat on the board of the Volkswagen Audi business in the UK.

He had enormous success in the role and in 1989 was asked to take over the car business when the incumbent retired. Richard viewed the role as a huge and exciting challenge. The car industry was not one in which he had maintained a close interest. He recognised that in taking the role he was moving from a part of the motor industry that was directly, personally customer motivated to an industry where one hardly ever saw, never mind knew, most of the customers. The VW and Audi business in the UK was characterised by an excellent product, sophisticated marketing and high spend. His position on the board had given him an insight into some of the issues at the Milton Keynes headquarters. It was a challenge he relished.

Thus he arrived in the role with an enviable track record of success, and a reputation for achievement. He believed in quality and service excellence, with customers clearly at the centre of everything. He valued integrity and professionalism, and trusted that, by and large, people in the company would do their best to do the right thing. He had strong self-reliance; an absolute belief that the customer is king; he was focused (he could be ruthless); he was willing and able to do the right thing; and he had a strong concern for people at all levels, and would look for the best in them and try to use their strengths. From a style perspective, he was a very private individual, guarding a clear separation between work and home, to the point where he could be seen as rude and therefore some people felt threatened because they found him very difficult to 'know'.

Many of the challenges he had faced up to now had involved inevitable change and been recognised as such. Although he had had to make change in the face of adversity, most of the barriers he had faced were from outside the organisation. He had yet to encounter the stultifying effect that personal agendas can have on a business and its ability to change.

At last, after 40 years, he had the opportunity of making a difference on a grand scale to the industry that he loved. Both his people and thought-leadership skills, as well as his own inner resources and ability to change himself, were about to be challenged on an unprecedented scale. He was about to discover that to make fundamental change happen, and more importantly stick, he himself would have to change.

He began his new role in the knowledge that VW Germany intended to buy back control of the UK business. The German parent company would clearly have expectations as to how they would wish to see Richard shape the business. And so, using tried and tested methods, he began his discovery phase. The high spots of the business were obvious, however, he found an organisation riding the crest of a wave of success but highly complacent about the future. There was little incentive or desire for any organisational learning – a flaw that could be potentially fatal in a rapidly changing marketplace.

I found a massive degree of self-satisfaction and a lack of strategic challenge. Our success to date had been built on the back of one or two super products, plus we had brilliant advertising. We thought our biggest problem was that we belonged to Lonrho. Actually it wasn't!... The problems were here inside this building. Volkswagen no longer occupied exclusive territory. We were moving to a free and open Europe, so what was the role of the importer anyway? Dealers were becoming less and less profitable and were increasingly cast in the role of servants to the Milton Keynes headquarters. Whether consciously or not we were setting dealer against dealer with huge volume bonuses, and we were selling to the same customers year after year, …and fewer and fewer of them. We had to sort out all these issues. It was clear to me that we could not sustain things as they were, something had to change. The top team was not working well together – this needed to be sorted out quickly. Most urgently, I needed to find a way of shaking the self-satisfaction out of the business and sending a very strong signal that we were in for a different regime after the years of stability.

Initiating the change

I have a very strong belief that the release of people, the management of people and their contribution are the key tasks in moving the business towards something different.

This belief in people and his instinct for action led him immediately to address the baronies that he found. At the time, there were strong functional silos, with favouritism, rather than meritocracy, being the norm. He began, with the help of a new personnel director, whom he had appointed himself, to introduce transparency in the personnel processes, to break the culture of favouritism and patronage. This laid important foundations for the future but was hugely resented. Richard's previous knowledge of the business, backed up by the discovery phase, had convinced him that the business was heading for a period where a major cost reduction exercise would be necessary, with the removal of significant chunks of fixed costs which, of course, would require compulsory redundancies. This would be for the first time in the history of the company. Richard decided, after much analysis, that a bold move was called for which would signal the coming of a new era and serve as a 'wake-up call' to the business. A 15 per cent compulsory cut in headcount across the organisation was prepared.

Ahead of this, Richard planned to present, to the entire organisation, a simple analysis of where the business stood and the challenges it faced as a consequence. This was intended to build ownership around the future. But it all went badly wrong and resulted in one of the low spots in

Richard's career, and created shock waves which still ripple through Milton Keynes today.

> Something very unfortunate happened [and here Richard colours heavily and drops his voice, losing his customary confidence] ...I wanted to talk personally to all the staff and their families and I wanted to try and explain why the world was changing. I wanted to try and set in people's minds the fact that we were going through a turbulent period. And it went about as badly wrong as is possible – the law of unintended consequences at work. I wanted to get the rough over and then begin the process of rebuilding the business.

The decision to hold the event was taken in the late summer and preparations placed in the hands of a very creative promotions department. The brief was to get as many families as possible to turn up on a Saturday afternoon, create a fun diversion for the children, and then separate the adults for the presentation. The 'fun diversion' turned out to be a big top with clowns and conjurers, tea and then a firework display over the lake to music by Handel. The turnout was huge and the event was spectacular.

But the extravaganza annihilated the message that things were supposed to be getting seriously tough. Second, the redundancy proposal had been in its early planning phase that summer and the thinking then was for a phased programme across the following year. During the autumn, however, it had been decided by the board to implement a one-off reduction early in December before families started spending for Christmas. But, due to the sensitivity of the subject, no one told the promotions department which continued blindly ahead with plans for the party. So Richard was seen to hoist storm cones and host an extravagant party in the same weekend, followed by the firing of 15 per cent of the employees just four weeks later.

> I didn't turn it off – I should have but I didn't – I didn't trust people here enough to say look, come on the inside, come into my confidence – this is going to happen between now and Christmas. If I had, I would have avoided the shock I created later, ...but, equally, I had just experienced a year when everything of a confidential nature I had discussed had been immediately broadcast!

Hence the celebration event happened and when, a few weeks later, in early December, the redundancies, which were to take immediate effect, were announced, the morale of the organisation went through the floor. In Richard's words it became:

an awful place to work... I was being heavily criticised... a lot of messages were going back to the factory in Wolfsberg saying there was a madman running the business. I hated coming in to work but you just have to get on with it. What is done is done. More than anything we needed a period of reasonable stability. But the feudal barons were still running their empires, nothing had changed and we simply had to address things if we were going to protect our future.

The baronies remained untouched, the initial process of change stalled at the first fence. Furthermore, Richard, at this stage, was still to form a clear picture of what the business might eventually look like. He was not able to stand out in front as the flag-carrying leader and challenge the barons with an alternative vision of the future – he had yet to find a mechanism to identify and unleash the change agents in a new direction. The organisation at this stage had no natural momentum of its own for change; there was no easy way to energise the organisation. Richard was struggling to find a leadership style that worked in this environment. 'The first time I stood up to address the organisation I was met by dumb insolence. I had always managed to get a tremendous contribution from people in previous businesses, it was being denied to me here... So what was wrong?'

He had no power base, no compelling vision yet with which to energise people, and no one else in the organisation apparently wanted change – he was the outsider. He was isolated from the business by the 'the Milton Keynes Broadcasting Corporation' – he could not get to the people he was supposed to lead. In addition, the 5 November debacle had cast Richard as the bad guy. His morale was low and his feelings were mixed. He was bewildered, he wondered why couldn't he get through, he tried to work out what was going on, was it him, was it the history, was it them? He felt huge grief at having caused the pain that the organisation was suffering. He felt anger that the top team did not see the need for change in the same way that he did.

Towards a new culture

In the immediate aftermath of 5 November, Richard fell back on analysis. He knew he needed to break up the power of the barons. He needed to find the managers who could cope with change. He brought in a couple of new players to the top team and gave each member of that team the benefit of the doubt. He believed in playing to strengths and neutralising weaknesses. In working through the problem with the head of personnel,

Richard conceded the need to break up sales and marketing as well as the old after-sales operation, and then put people into the newly created boxes. This was an extremely tough period for Richard. He was under pressure from all quarters; Germany, the board, the market and the organisation. He was searching around trying to find something that would work. Using his previous experience, he tried all sorts of rational levers – textbook stuff – most of which were analytically driven. He did not at this point attack the top-down people issue head-on. Rather, he tried to inject momentum into the business, hoping to create change from the bottom up. At the same time, his thinking about what the future could look like was slowly beginning to emerge. Part of the reorganisation included the set-up of the logistics function – this move gave birth and opportunity for practical learning to the concept of the lean enterprise.

The new 'boxes' resulting from the reorganisation created opportunities for the employees to decide whether they were part of the past or the future – 'people started to cross the floor'. Richard at last started to build a franchise, a direct route and voice into the organisation, outside the influence of the board. He began to develop visibility and build a reality to counter the myth. He began to create his own space and personality in the organisation. The old Milton Keynes Broadcasting Corporation (the informal, anecdotal communication system within the baronies) began to be challenged. With the new structure in place, the organisation started to slough off the old corporate personality, a new one slowly started to emerge and a new culture began to appear. Richard was taking the first steps in changing things, albeit rationally driven. However, as progress on a day-to-day basis slowly began, Richard's confidence began to return. As his confidence grew, he started to spend less time focused on the here and now, and more on thinking through what the future could look like.

At about this time, towards the end of 1992, Richard began to think about what would happen if he had the opportunity to set up a totally new importer business. How would he organise a business set-up from scratch? He was quickly able to start blue skying what it might look like – free to creatively and imaginatively shape the organisation. This he found surprisingly easy, because there were neither personal relationships nor personal emotions clogging any part of the business. The shackles were taken away. This was a revelation to Richard, and led to the undeniable fact that the barrier to change he was currently facing was a cultural one. Richard knew he needed to do something in this area, but he was not sure what. He was ready to understand what would seriously change the way things were. He went outside to various consultancies and, after a 'beauty parade', Philip Keslake of Raeburn-Keslake was introduced to the organisation. Keslake was the right person at the right time – he and Richard immediately connected. Rather than coming in with 'canned' solutions, he worked with Richard to understand what exactly was the issue the organisation faced. In parallel, he helped Richard to understand which of his own behaviours stifled progress and which behaviours facilitated it, that is, what he should stop doing and what he should do more of. Through this process, Philip Keslake moved Richard away from being hands-on with everything on a day-to-day basis, and encouraged him to become more of a facilitator/coach to the organisation. At the same time, he helped Richard adapt his style to become less distant, and show more of his personality, and not simply play the role, to the organisation.

The road to Damascus

With Philip's help, Richard was beginning to undergo a personal transformation and starting to address the cultural issues. Philip described Richard as being like King Arthur with his Round Table. Things were moving; 'was it me?' was starting to change; 'was it them?', Richard was getting to know the organisation better and they him; 'was it history?', he was beginning to focus on the individuals. A case was being built to do something which could at last start to chip away at the root causes which were adversely affecting the organisation's ability to change.

In parallel to the work Keslake was doing with Richard, a similar process was being run with the rest of the board. Each member of the board was described by his colleagues in terms of strengths and weaknesses. These were shown, unattributed, in an open forum to the whole board. Everyone learned through looking in the mirror, forcing a recognition of the reality of how the individuals were seen by others; it put a number of things on a knife edge and created an unstoppable momentum. There were a number of shocks here for the individuals. Things had to happen. It created a situation where there was no going back. From a business perspective, this process facilitated some critical unblocking moves, the business was no longer a top-down organisation; the old guard was changing. From an emotional and individual perspective, a number of things were left dangling. With simultaneous and dramatic changes happening in the marketplace and pressure increasing from competitors, customers and dealers, there was a perfect coming together of deficit and aspiration which created an ideal environment for change. On a personal level, it was a time of huge excitement and growth for Richard. He was learning how to add value in the new role, how to begin to address the issues of the future, how to become more accessible to his team, while continuing to develop his idea as to what a new future could look like. At the same time, the organisation was learning that things could be different and things did need to change. Most importantly, they were beginning to recognise that Richard, as their leader, could be trusted to drive these changes through. In fact, the whole period was a road to Damascus for the organisation. The culture change programme was a critical catalyst; with one of the key outputs being the transformation of Richard himself.

Working together for personal transformation

Philip Keslake won Richard's trust upfront; there was an immediate empathy between the two of them. Keslake demonstrated he was prepared to listen, to understand what was wanted and then to shape something that made sense. He did not try to be too analytical, but used enough data to make things real and useable and then provided support when needed. This approach was useful and practical and in no way superficial. The output provided data that confirmed a number of Richard's intuitions; this in turn built the trust between the two men to allow them to work together on changing Richard's leadership style. It has been said a number of times that the culture change programme had one key output – the transformation of one man. Together Richard and Philip put in place a virtuous circle that facilitated major organisational change. Having established credibility through his work with the board, Philip had earned the right to coach Richard. Keslake listened to Richard and reflected back to him what he heard; he held up the mirror as to how Richard was impacting on the organisation. Richard was able to recognise this image and his commitment to changing the organisation fuelled the will to do something about it. He had the courage to change and Keslake was able to tell him how. In addition, through the work he was doing with the rest of the organisation, Keslake had built up enough trust to persuade them to give Richard the room to change – to get the organisation to 'try him and see'. Richard was able, through a different set of demonstrated behaviours, to present his emerging vision and to build an excitement for it – to provide a momentum for the business to both believe in something different for the future and, crucially, in Richard as the individual who could lead them to it. By transforming himself, Richard had unblocked the organisation. Additionally, as he presented his vision, it started to develop and grow and eventually to take on a life of its own. During this process, Richard made a significant shift away from managing the business to leading it – he began to move away from the flag-carrying upfront planner with his fingers on all the day-

to-day details to becoming much more action-learning focused. He began to step back and coach the organisation rather than providing the answer. In his words: 'I would paint the landscape – they would fill in the trees, rivers and other details.'

Philip Keslake was the key catalyst. He was able to provide Richard with the right tools at the right time and support him through his change. His reflections on Richard at the time are revealing. On seeing the board in action early on in the relationship, he saw Richard very much as Arthur presiding over the Round Table – a powerful and somewhat isolated figure. He was extremely impressed by, if somewhat in awe of, Richard's passion, commitment and vision.

Brand separation

Richard began to sense how his ambition of leaving a legacy and creating change could combine, and he was beginning to see what he had to do to make it happen. In his mind the initial idea of brand separation, separating out Audi and Volkswagen, emerged. At this time the German parent company did not allow him to pursue this strategy. Then another big break, the regime in Germany changed and Piech was appointed to the chief executive role. Richard began to work on brand separation seriously. The concept in his mind was of empowering the brand businesses, of giving them as much autonomy as they possibly could have, with as much freedom and authority as necessary to support it. He designed the organisation structure first and foremost and then put people into boxes. This exercise Richard undertook alone, taking only Phil Pavard, the HR manager, into his confidence. In thinking through the issue in this way, a number of things became clear. Once no longer constrained by the incumbent managers and their agendas, it became obvious that the future organisation could not work with one of the old directors in any of the new roles – he simply did not fit the new future. Because of his personality and track record, he would be the wrong person to run one of the new businesses. Displacing one of the key existing barons fundamentally influenced the shape of the future organisation.

Holding up the mirror – an internal conscience

In all his time at Volkswagen, indeed in his entire career, Richard very much kept his own counsel. Only at two points in his career, both during the transformation process, did Richard develop relationships with coaches or confidantes who were then able to work with him to support and help to shape his personal and business transformation.

On the more technical front, in moving Richard from viewing the senior people issue as 'a constraint within which he had to work' to seeing them as barriers which could be overcome, and which could therefore facilitate his emerging vision for the extended enterprise, Phil Pavard was critical.

Although initially, following the departure of his 'own' personnel director, Richard did not immediately view Phil as the natural successor for the role, he quickly came to value him and took him into his confidence. Phil took over the personnel role when things were at their most difficult for Richard. Richard was isolated from the business and the power of the barons was undiminished. His vision as to what the business could look like had begun to emerge, but he was still shackled by the challenges posed by the personalities and styles of the existing management team. In working through with Phil what the organisational structure could look like, Phil was able to hold up the mirror to Richard and get him to finally acknowledge the need to address this situation. With his professional knowledge, Phil was able to help Richard to think through the ramifications of such a step and plan the most appropriate way of facilitating the changes. Through his professional relationships with the individuals involved, Phil propositioned the changes and thereby helped to ease the process of separation.

Although not close in personal terms, Richard and Phil have a strong and enduring professional relationship, unique in Richard's career. The relationship is based on deep mutual respect and a shared values system. Phil is somewhat unusual for an HR man. He has a degree in law backed by a strong track record in industrial relations. He is absolutely focused on doing the right thing for the organisation, sometimes almost to the point of ruthlessness. He is not encumbered with a large ego and is therefore able to be and remain highly objective. He is clear-sighted about people and assesses their strengths and weaknesses well. He is able to deliver difficult messages without flinching or ducking the issues, and he is an accurate communicator applying little or no filtering to the original message. He is discrete, has high integrity and is unquestioningly loyal to his leader. In short, he was the perfect sounding board for Richard.

The relationship between Phil and Richard worked because of their shared commitment to people and to their preferred personal style. Richard knew and valued intuitively the people, yet did not fully have the technical skills to unleash and implement his beliefs – Phil provided this input. Furthermore, Phil acted as a conscience to Richard on people issues. He said things that struck a chord with Richard, in an objective way such that Richard could hear, and subsequently think about handling. He did not let Richard off the hook and consequently made him step up to the need for action.

Delivering transformation

It was a powerful partnership in which they shared similar drivers (excellence, a desire to make a difference and a focus on people not personal gain), similar styles and similar values (discretion, trust and integrity and a preference to keep their own counsel). The work they did together was undoubtedly critical in driving the success of the transformation.

This was an exciting time, putting the pieces together, thinking through the art of the possible, but it was not without risk. Richard had a choice – duck the tough decision and put the future and his legacy at risk or bite the bullet and think the unthinkable. 'It was a huge risk. But the alternative – either face the risk then or face sitting here today with a thoroughly incompetent, uncompetitive business. So when do you take this risk? You take it when you have a chance of recovery.'

Decisions around people are always the toughest to take. However, there was no walking away from the decision. This did not make it any easier, 'however much you think about the right answer... and you do. You agonise, you seriously bloody agonise over it.' But it had to be done, and with the support of Phil Pavard, arrangements were made for the director to leave the business. This was a huge shock, both for the individual and for the organisation. Having had the news broken to him, he packed his desk and left the building within half an hour. Subsequently he has never worked in the mainstream automotive industry. This was another tough time, but by now Richard had the confidence and full support of Germany:

> They were totally behind me. They were there when I needed them. We had done some pretty adventurous things already in stripping down, going lean, outsourcing and restructuring operations, going through huge people changes, and the culture work with Keslake. These things all fitted into a pattern of change that was not going on anywhere else in the Volkswagen world – it was absolutely new. But still we had the lowest market share in Europe and I know that they would have sacrificed me if they had lost faith in me – and they must have been pretty close to it at times. So I realised that I may go out with the bath water – but I had to accept that and keep going.

Having designed the new organisation with Phil Pavard and decided how best to fill the top positions, the vision moved to its next phase. All the senior and middle management, about 80 people in total, were brought together in a single room on a Monday morning to talk through the implications of implementing the brand-based businesses. The entire organisation was designed and agreed in that single day. The team sat at round tables, Richard gave them the rationale, the whys and the principles of what he was trying to do. They were then invited to ask questions. The room, not surprisingly, was full of questions; Richard was walking around the tables answering them off the cuff. He was now doing what his instinct had told him to do at the outset of his tenure in Milton Keynes. This was a real high point for Richard, a turning point after a number of years in the doldrums:

> The worst was over and we were coming back – there was no question of that! They loved the idea of what we would do and fired a myriad of questions. If there was one I couldn't answer. I said, 'park it'. As the day went on, all the unanswered questions were farmed out and they worked on them and came back with recommendations. We had the whole organisation fixed by six o'clock that night – everything – we just went and did it, including how to make first-quarter targets. Later we followed this with a live satellite show to the dealers.

This was a major milestone in changing the direction and shape of the business. Richard reaffirmed his own personal contract, reminding himself that the brand was everything. In real terms, this meant the brand heads would have the power and authority to run their own businesses, while he would merely facilitate and move away from day-to-day operations to more of a chairman-type role. He had the finance, legal, dealer ventures and HR department reporting directly to him. The Group itself became less and less visible to the public, all the power went to the brands, and as this happened Richard's role became very different. It was a period of huge change.

> It was rather like watching your children leave. Eventually they do come back, but there is a period when they move off and they very deliberately don't want anything to do with you. As the brands took power, it felt as if they were tearing themselves away from mother earth and ditching mother earth in order to create their own space. It was a great feeling but it did create another set of issues.

During this phase, Phil Pavard, who continued to work closely with Richard, found himself continually surprised by the emerging vision. 'Richard's ambitions for the organisation were very stretching.'

So the Group moved into its next phase of development. A number of the brands wanted to create total independence and for a period of time went through a phase that drove duplication and risked losing the synergies and benefits that the Group represented. The conversation then moved, guided by Richard, to debate: 'So you have separate dealers, you have a separate identity, you have separate products. What does that mean to the customer? What is the value we are delivering to them?' Soon came another real test for Richard's leadership. His new management team had been recruited, including some new leaders from outside the business, and put in place with a specific brief to build the brands. They set about their new tasks with enthusiasm and a not insignificant degree of success in the marketplace – soon the brands were very definitely king. Yet what the management team as a whole failed to see was that they were actually duplicating efforts and thereby detracting from the overall value of the Group; in many cases there was very little real differentiation between the brands.

Audi dealers were nothing of the sort, they were all Volkswagen dealers with a piece of Elastoplast over their badge and four rings biroed in instead! They were all so busy focusing on their brand, they didn't really have time to think about the broader picture. 'Eyes down – don't disturb me – I've got enough on at my plate.' There was a huge amount of management time being spent which had no differentiated benefit to the customer at all. And it was all extremely complicated, unnecessarily so – and to top it all IT was in a mess.

The final phase

Despite coaching from the background, Richard could not get it to register on anyone's agenda that the duplication and complication was something they had to deal with. Technically, the concept in his mind was very difficult, and, therefore, communicating it in a way which made sense to all the diverse players was immensely tough. He had to miss a board of management meeting when the issue was on the agenda, but in his absence it was dismissed and he knew at that point that his team considered the issue to be unimportant – and, more importantly, by implication, considered his role to be unimportant.

I had in mind the concept of the extended enterprise as a planetary system and how you actually made it work. I was very, very absorbed with how you developed such a structure and how you made it work. How you could balance a brand-based business through independent dealers, and deliver a brand promise to customers.

His vision was once again under threat. For some time there was every likelihood that the Group he had worked so hard to turn around would spin off into a number of separate brand businesses which would not be able to capitalise on the strength of the Group or optimise the opportunities to be had from synergies. Richard had unleashed a business which was having huge success in the marketplace but which was failing to achieve against the vision he had so painstakingly developed for it. He now entered a another period of intense frustration. This was a period of enormous difficulty for him, the temptation was to slip back into his old style of command and control and say, 'we will do it like this'. But he recognises that had he done so, he might just as well have walked out of the business – 'it needed some real soul searching to work out how to do it without reverting to command and control' – however, had he done this it would have spoiled everything, his vision would become impossible, so he had to bite his tongue. Furthermore, he knew that although he had developed the vision, he could not and should not paint in the details himself.

I knew that I couldn't work it out myself – I had no right to work it out. It wasn't an admission of failure, it was a recognition of leadership as it should be. As you go through your early career, you get promoted because you are pretty smart, and you are pretty smart because you make some damn good decisions. You make these decisions in context because you are close to the customer. Most business decisions are ones that affect your customers, and you believe as you progress up the management ladder that that is what you are good at and therefore that is what you do. But increasingly, of course, you are doing this out of context, because you are getting further and further away from the customer. Then you shouldn't take these decisions at all, but rather pass them to people closer to the markct. That is the trick of leadership, identifying who is best equipped to take the decisions and empowering them to do so.

However doing this in practice is extremely hard and in Richard's words: 'this was a period of deep depression, the same facing up to failure, of getting it wrong, of having an enduring determination not to give up and trying to understand why things were not going the way I wanted them to.' Typically, he spent an enormous amount of time working on the problem, and slowly he began to realise 'the problem wasn't them, it was me, because I couldn't explain what was in my mind in a way that found a corresponding picture in their minds. So the issue became how to bring the pictures together.'

Once again a huge amount of time was spent working with the board of management, getting them to understand the next phase of the vision which was centred on a major initiative synergising processes and systems across the enterprise. Eventually, the penny started to drop and a move was made to communicate this across the entire organisation. But still the management team failed to understand their role in moving it forward; they wanted somebody else to put everything right for them. The root of the problem was getting people to understand how to communicate with each other. Richard put together a team called PAS (Processes and Systems), whose brief was to work on this issue and understand how best to build synergies across the Group and its dealer networks. The team consisted of a small number of young up-and-comers from across the brands. They were given freedom as to how to address the issue and subsequently brought in a team of consultants to help them.

Richard, through his own creation, had to watch their progress from the sideline. 'The result is, of course, terribly frustrating... but equally the result is serious power, serious energy, commitment and ownership right across the organisation from top to bottom, because suddenly people begin see how they can contribute.' Over the course of the next 18 months, from mid-1997 onwards, the organisation began to grasp firmly onto Richard's vision – everything coalesced back into a vision of what the business was really about, what the added value was, how it created a superior customer experience, how to differentiate the business, and finally where the systems and processes fitted in to all of this. The result is the business that sits in Milton Keynes today – a leading edge extended enterprise – and to quote Richard 'a joyous place to be'.

Reflections

Having spent time reflecting back on the journey at Volkswagen, Richard talked about some of his key learnings.

What really makes change happen?

You must be brutally honest about what the business really is and what its strengths are. This requires accurate benchmarking and clear analysis in order to understand the competitive situation. This helps to define the art of the possible. It is also a first step in getting people to recognise what it is that they are *not* good at and what therefore they may need help at. Once you can begin to work out how to put 'that' right, you can begin to plan the way ahead and start to execute this step by step. ...As the business begins to make progress, the early obstacles start to go away – you create a virtuous circle. As progress proceeds, you start to find those people who feel comfortable with change and a hunger is generated in them – the pace then begins to quicken. The realisation dawns on you, and on them, that you can do anything you want to if you work hard enough at it, and think carefully enough about it! ...No one who is successful is successful by accident.

What is leadership?

In my younger days I had seen leadership as grabbing a flag, running with it and leading from out front; consulting yes, listening yes, but essentially taking over the decision-making. That can work, but it means the business is built around, and dependent on, you. Sustain-ability of your vision beyond your tenure is by no means certain.

If, however, you make sure that people understand their role *and* how the whole thing fits together, you begin to get massively improved decision-making. Your role as leader then becomes quite different; it becomes a questioning, ambition-creating role.

Once I'd understood what was required of me, I had to make it a reality. I had to give up doing things; be very determined to largely disappear from the organisation structure.

Today my role is very different again – my role is to work out how, as a business, we can differentiate, how we can become more competi-tive. To help me do this, I developed a clear picture of what the world would look like, asking what would we like to do that we can't do today. I challenge my team to think about this. I try to ask the impos-sible, and to ask it in a way that irritates, in a way which requires scratching at. I keep pushing and little by little someone has a good idea... I have to ask the impossible question, they have to give the answer.

Leadership is about getting the right people in the right places; it is thought-leadership around people. My goal has been to have super businesses peopled by super people.

It is difficult to lead a business unless you are prepared to be an equal and open member of the business – you have to be prepared to sacrifice yourself to the business.

My understanding of leadership and what it takes has changed. This has been influenced by a number of factors. First, by adversity – the sheer difficulty of it. Second, by my immediate colleagues, what they have said, notably Phil Pavard and Philip Keslake. Third, by frustration, the frustration of not being able to easily get where I wanted to be – it frustrated the hell out of me! I spent HUGE amounts of time thinking about it – it dominated me – it still does!

Looking back, what would you do differently?

Looking particularly at the early days at Volkswagen, I would want to see if I could communicate things better, particularly around the need for change; I'd wish to handle it in a less abrupt way... I did not handle it well.

I would be better at drawing blurry pictures, and let other people fill in the details. I would have hoped for better pictures and therefore better communication earlier. At a couple of key points, the first tranche of cost cutting, the set-up of processes and systems – I would have wanted to communicate that better – I don't think I did that well.

What have been the greatest influences on you?

Undoubtedly my parents. They were always there as a safety net, but they treated me as a competent adult from my earliest days. I absorbed a huge amount from them. Their philosophy was 'don't just talk about it, do it'. This meant that the luxury of just being able to talk about something was denied. By the time I was in my early 20s, I had achieved a lot and done a lot, both inside and outside work. I was hugely self-reliant and absolutely determined that failure was not on the agenda.

On the negative side, I was strongly influenced by the real world of running dealerships. I became angry at the amateurship in the industry; it just didn't equate with the standards I set myself. But you can't just criticise, you must do something, and so I started to think seriously about the yawning gap between what it was and what I thought it should be. It then took me 40 years to get to the point where I could make a difference on a large enough scale. On the way there were some key stimuli; INSEAD, and the experience at Lex (Trevor Chin in particular) were some key beacons.

People who I most admire and who have therefore influenced me include Ernest Shackleton. I would have loved to be him – the man who took his ship into the Arctic ice, lost his ship but saved every single man in appalling conditions with no idea what was going to happen next. I find it enormously powerful as a parable.

8 Tim Waterstone

The business story

Tim Waterstone started a revolution in the British book retail trade when he founded Waterstone's in 1982 with a loan of £10,000 from his father-in-law. By 1998, when Tim became chairman of HMV Media, Waterstone's, which by now included rival Dillons, had a turnover of £390 million from 208 shops, four million customers and 22 per cent of the bookselling market.

The transformation of bookselling was such that by 1995 Nick Hornby, himself a bestselling author, was asking in *The Spectator*, 'Whatever did we do before Waterstone's?'

The arrival of Waterstone's not only changed the way books were sold in Britain, but it is also credited with founding the fortunes of some publishing houses, such as Faber and Faber and Bloomsbury, and even of individual authors such as Louis de Bernières and Frank McCourt, who were protégés of Waterstone's.

In fact, before the arrival of Waterstone's, books were sold either through uninviting, badly laid out, specialist shops, where modern merchandising techniques were regarded with great suspicion, or through chains such as WHSmith and Menzies, where books had to compete for floor space with stationery and newspapers. In fact, in the early 1980s Smiths had announced that they were planning to reduce their dependence on books from 25 per cent of turnover to 15 per cent.

Neither the specialist nor the chains stocked more than the minimum range of mass-market titles, relying on a cumbersome process of ordering single copies of anything more rarified from publishers via their local wholesaler. Neither invited the browser, and staff were generally considerably less well read than customers. Even if you knew what you wanted when you entered, actually finding it required some luck and determination. There was absolutely no chance of leaving with something that had just caught your eye.

What Tim Waterstone did was to create an environment in which people could indulge their love for books, where entering a bookshop became a pleasurable experience in itself, rather than a gauntlet to be run. He introduced bigger shops, with space to walk around and proper layout. These shops carry a larger range of titles, typically around 50,000 are always in stock; are open for longer hours; and are staffed by people, often graduates, who have actually read the title you are looking for, and may well be writing their own book in between serving customers.

Tim Waterstone opened the first of these shops in the Old Brompton Road in September 1982, after having been sacked by WHSmith. In fact, the story of Waterstone's is thoroughly entwined with that of WHSmith. Tim had joined the company in 1973 and had been fired by Simon Hornby for supposedly failing to succeed with a publishing venture in New York. In a classic 'your job or mine' scenario, Tim carried the can, but gained with it an enthusiasm for retailing when Hornby suggested that Smiths would rather he didn't open a bookshop.

The first shop was successful, and was quickly followed by one in Charing Cross Road, opened with the help of Christina Foyle. And then one in Southampton Row, and then Regent Street, and so on, as fast as cash would allow and sites could be found. Key concerns were to get the right people running the branches, since there was no hierarchy – all promotions were from within – and to keep raising money.

By 1989, there were 31 shops, and the business was heavily borrowed as interest rates rose. Waterstone judged that there was sufficient risk of the high street turning negative to respond favourably to an offer from WHSmith for 50 per cent of the company for a price of £42 million. The press reported that Tim stood to receive £9 million personally, which included an extra £1 million to compensate for the firing seven years before.

There followed a period of four years over which the earn-out took place, at the end of which Waterstone's was turning over £130 million and making a profit of £10 million. Smiths had brought with them Sheratt & Hughes which was integrated over a three-year period, nearly doubling the size of the operation.

In 1993, Tim Waterstone left the business to pursue, among other things, a career as a novelist. In 1997, he opened a new retail vision, a children's department store called Daisy & Tom, and that autumn was prompted by WHSmith's poor performance and succession problems to make a debt-financed bid of over £1 billion for the whole of the WHSmith group. The bid was rejected, but did result in a reorganisation by WHSmith which included a demerger of Waterstone's.

Tim Waterstone put together a consortium, worth around £800 million, with EMI and a venture capitalist, Advent International, which acquired the 106 Waterstone's branches, EMI's 78 Dillons outlets and 271 HMV music shops.

In autumn 1999, the company opened its 70,000 square feet Piccadilly store, the biggest bookshop in Europe, with five miles of shelves and 270,000 titles, but by the middle of that year, after the first year of trading, the new company showed a loss of £21 million in a worsening retail market. With the added threat of increased competition, not least from Borders, the American bookseller, the new operational management at Waterstone's sought major cost savings and increased centralisation of decision-making. This resulted in press stories of a crisis in staff morale over the loss of branch autonomy and traditional values, amid fears that Waterstone's was 'dumbing down' in order to spread its target market. At the end of 1999, Tim was reported in the press to be considering a bid to buy back the chain from HMV Media.

Tim's background and career path

The youngest son of a tea-planter, who had left school at 14, Tim was educated at Tonbridge School and, although considered the dunderhead of the family in comparison with his older sister and brother, succeeded in getting into Cambridge, where he read English. He married shortly after leaving university and went to India, where his family had been missionaries for generations.

Having caught typhoid, he returned to England after a year and eventually joined Allied Breweries in 1964 as a trainee, where he worked for Sir Derrick Holden-Brown. He joined WHSmith in 1973, and was eventually sent to America to start the publishing venture which was the cause of his departure from Smiths three years later.

Stage one: building Waterstone's

The inspiration for the vision that was to transform the UK book trade was Tim being fired by WHSmith for failing to deliver the business plan he was supposed to perform in America. It was a plan that he believes was undeliverable, but he was still held responsible. Looking back on the experience, he says: 'It was a gruesome firing. I was actually outraged, it was so unfair. It was an outrageous piece of "fire the next man down". In those days Smiths was very centrist, extremely upper class, and totally unmeritocratic.'

Tim had already spotted the trend toward large format literary book-selling in the US and brought it to Smiths' attention as possibly relevant to the UK. When Simon Hornby suggested that Smiths would prefer it if Tim, having been fired, did not open a chain of bookshops, the connection was obvious.

But Tim had to go through a year-and-a-half of 'absolute nightmare' before he could get the idea off the ground. Back in the UK, his London house was literally collapsing, and he had to put most of his redundancy pay into shoring it up. He was partially separated from his second wife and now had six children to support. As a result he was, he says in retrospect, 'not a million miles away from a nervous breakdown'.

The turning point came when Tim was confronted by the 'spirit of human defeat' of a dole queue in Wandsworth, and walked out of the Labour Exchange, vowing not to give in, and to make the Waterstone's idea a reality.

His anger at the treatment by Smiths was further fuelled by the contempt he was met with when trying to raise finance. Contempt which, he feels, was encouraged by Smiths trying to discourage potential investors. And contempt which he associated with an unmeritocratic system.

However, after the Labour Exchange epiphany, Tim was now possessed by a huge determination: 'What wore everybody down at the end of the day was absolutely staggering determination, and it just battered down the banks, battered down the people putting up the money, it battered down Smiths ultimately.' In addition to his father-in-law's £10,000, he got a little bit of money from 3i, secured a £100,000 loan from the bank, and opened up in Old Brompton Road.

To take Waterstone's from being a good idea into reality required considerable determination. Not just to build a business, but also to repair the damage done by getting fired: 'I did have an absolutely raw determination – beyond determination, an obsession – to build up a really good business, and I guess to build up recognition for myself. I would wake up several times in the night all the time thinking about how to drive it on.'

Smiths not only provided Tim with the initial inspiration, his feelings toward them were a constant spur: 'I did absolutely despise them, so some of my drive was directed actually at making fools of them. Similarly Richard Branson with British Airways, and Bill Gates with IBM. You do have enemies that you aim at, and they are generally big corporations.'

The Waterstone's concept proved immediately popular and, between 1982 and 1989, 30 shops were opened, with Smiths unwittingly providing Waterstone's with a branch strategy: 'Once we got our confidence up, we used to open as close as possible (to a WHSmith branch). Preferably one beside and one across the street from it.'

Expansion was pursued as fast as cash would allow: 'As soon as we got a pound we opened a branch,' says Tim, and the next seven years were spent in a blur of activity finding sites, opening branches and continually raising finance.

Not that the business was yet making a profit – targets were often missed – but Tim's determination was based on a self-belief that bordered on arrogance. 'You've got to have absolutely unshakeable self-belief: if you have that it spills over to everybody – the staff, the public and the bank managers.' Tim was quite clear that, since browsing in bookshops was one of his own favourite things, there must be a few million people out there like himself.

But to build it into a significant business, whatever the provocation from Smiths, indicates a considerable contempt for risk. Although he says that he personally needs the element of risk: 'I do like to be on the edge of danger work-wise', and that an entrepreneur has to be prepared to mortgage everything if necessary, 'you should nevertheless never tell your wife about the risk or she will walk out on you immediately'.

During that period of initial expansion, the public growth of Waterstone's, the distinctive bookshop, was paralleled by the internal development of Waterstone's, the distinctive organisation.

The latter had several key features. First, there was virtually no organisation structure. It had just two levels: Tim (who was both chairman and chief executive), and then the branches. This was a deliberate policy in order to keep decision-making in the branches. There book-buying was pushed out to the junior booksellers, which had the double benefit of improving the inventory and encouraging a sense of ownership among the staff. The other benefit of having just two levels was that lines of communication were very direct, a great asset when you just have to deliver.

Tim found it easy to operate in this way: 'I did naturally like delegating to people, but actually what happened is that I didn't have time to do anything else. I had some smashing people join me on day one, all from Hatchards, and the easiest thing to do was to give them control.'

The culture was deliberately non-corporate – Tim talks of 'building a bit of a family around the company'. As befitted an upmarket, literary retailer, the kind of people who Waterstone's wanted to attract, and did attract in their hundreds, were book people who would feel that they had never really left their undergraduate common rooms. When recruiting, Tim invited them to leave if they started to find it all boring, but they mostly became caught up by his fervour, found the whole thing fun and stayed.

From the earliest days, promotion was from within, thereby offering some growth prospects in a flat structure, and preserving the gene pool. It was also driven by Tim's determination to create in his own company the meritocratic culture he had found so missing in the Smiths and Allied Breweries of his earlier career, and one in which people could enjoy what they did, rather than being motivated solely by their mortgage.

One of his personal values which Tim sought to foster in the organisation was openness. Speaking of relationships with shareholders in the early days, he says: 'Everybody knew we risked everything every five minutes, but went with it. We used to have board meetings every two weeks or so. I do believe passionately in actually telling the truth all the time.'

Similarly, with Christina Foyle, who had offered Tim the Charing Cross Road site right at the beginning. 'I said "It is extremely nice of you, but I haven't got any money." She said "How much rent can you afford to pay?" and I said "To be completely honest, nothing."' The result was a critical six-month rent postponement.

The same spirit underlay the relationships with the business's other key suppliers, the publishers, who were effectively providing much of the working capital through credit. The value of supplier partnering is now much better understood, but the Waterstone's approach sounds as though it was based on an emotional bond as much as on good business sense. Tim talks of the interconnectedness of publishing and bookselling, and of how he feels 'comfort' and 'empathy' with publishers.

The fact that mutual confidence was required helped Waterstone's to negotiate very long credit terms, but they then had to ensure that, rather than abusing the terms they had been given, care was taken to make sure that payment did take place. Or that, on the rare occasion when there was going to be any sort of delay, great pains were taken to communicate with the publisher concerned ahead of time, and to be specific as to when payment would be made.

All these relationships, whether with shareholders, suppliers or other forms of partner, had to based on trust, which is certainly increased by shared risk, but depends also on intimacy, the ability to be open, to be yourself.

Tim had no problem in taking the leadership role. He says of himself: 'I do have a big ego,' and he told a journalist: 'I love companies when I am running them. I like the leadership. I'm a pretty ungenerous employee, if I feel the direction of the company is wrong.'

He is quite clear that getting that direction right is the leader's role, and that the health of the organisation depends on it: 'Businesses are most happily led when you have absolutely clear direction.'

But leading a company that you have started yourself, and which carries your own name, is a different form of leadership. Tim's view is that: 'It is a form of leadership that is very, very different to the professional leader.

There is no dividing line between you and the business, and that must communicate very directly to the people that work there.'

This creates a very personal, and reciprocal, relationship between the leader and those who work in the business, with strong parallels in the family. The employees want to 'belong' to the leader, to 'be looked after' and to share his vision. The leader, in turn, has 'to put his arms around his own people'.

One result of the personal nature of this relationship is that there are high levels of mutual commitment. The corollary, however, is that, if anything happens to disrupt the relationship, it can feel like rejection and be very painful.

Tim says: 'What my enemies say about me are two things – that I have ruthlessness, and I never know what that means, and that I show favouritism. When I first read someone saying that in the press, I was very taken aback, but then I did recognise the truth. I think that what it means is that I'm very attracted by people who have got a real sort of drive and some guts. I think that you have got to win for your team. It is true that if people are not in the right job, I do get rid of them, but of course that is because I think the team has to be protected.'

Given his own experience with Smiths, 'being got rid of' is something with dark overtones for Tim. The part of him that wants things for the business to be absolutely right can say briskly: 'We had numerous financial directors in the early days', but then he displays some of the personal cost of making the necessary changes, by confessing to a journalist that the guilt still makes him feel sick over having once had to sack an assistant manager at Waterstone's who went on to have a full-blown nervous breakdown.

Although he is very confident in his own ability to measure people's capacities, often intuitively, he still needs the reassurance that he has done the right thing: 'If you are instinctively good at measuring people's capacity, it is reassuring when you move someone out of a job, and when they position themselves where they should be, you see how much happier they are. People do get out of synch with their own capacity, and it's a great relief to reposition them. The only golden key about the whole thing is that you have to be incredibly generous financially.'

Stage two: the sale to WHSmith

Between 1982 and 1989, the strategy for Waterstone's had been growth rather than profitability. The concept worked, there was a gap in the market, so go for market share. The only barriers to growth were the availability of suitable sites and sufficient funds. Growth provided the opportunities to promote from within, and with a decentralised organisation, adding stores did not necessarily increase the need for resources at the centre.

However, by 1989 the high street went really badly wrong, and, with Waterstone's being heavily over-borrowed, Tim was afraid that it would not survive a prolonged period of depressed sales: 'It really did look awful out there, and what I was terrified of was Waterstone's going under. We probably wouldn't have done, but I didn't want to throw the whole thing away.'

WHSmith approached Waterstone and offered to buy 50 per cent of the company for a guaranteed £42 million. Whatever his feelings about selling out, let alone selling out to the hated WHSmith, Tim's priority was the survival of what he had created. Of course, it wasn't as simple as that – WHSmith offered to bring with them Sheratt & Hughes, which would nearly double the size of Waterstone's. And Tim did stand to realise considerable value from his own shareholding, which cannot have been immaterial for a man who once said: 'Concern about having enough money dogged me for twenty years.'

But there was something very poetic about being approached by Smiths, whatever the price: 'Having fired me, it was a slight irony, which I did milk to death. I stuck a million on the price, and I said to them "There, that's for the insult", which, to their credit, they did accept.'

Although there were good business reasons to make the sale, it was clearly a decision that caused Tim pain as well. He later said: 'I hated the selling out', and compared the emotional impact to that described by Sir Richard Branson when he sold Virgin Music to Thorn EMI. In *Losing My Virginity* (Virgin, 1998), Branson has written that, after addressing the staff of Virgin Music, 'I left the room and set off down Ladbroke Grove, tears streaming down my face.'

To Tim, those feelings were instantly recognisable. In talking about Branson's experience, he says: 'That was me, that was me.'

The break, although painful, was not to be clean. The deal with WHSmith was that they would buy up the remaining shares in Waterstone's over a three- or four-year period, with a guaranteed minimum price. During that time, Tim was working up the value in the company, which eventually reached £53 million, and was very much left alone by the new owner: 'They were so petrified of me that I never saw them. But to give them their due, it was smartly done as well. Complete non-interference.'

During that time, Waterstone's had to integrate the 18 or so Sheratt & Hughes shops, which was a very difficult process because of the differences in culture and operations. At the branch level, the staff were keen to 'do a Waterstone's', but there was some resistance in middle management.

It took longer than it should have to integrate, and in retrospect Tim feels that: 'We were a little bit indecisive about it.'

But by 1992, it was beginning to feel much better and by 1993 the results were very good. That was the year that WHSmith finally bought out the rest of the shares, and the original shareholders, who had bought in at 10p, sold at £5.28. By the time that Tim left in 1993, the sales were £130 million, and the combined business was making a profit of £10 million.

As the business grew, it had began to develop more of a management structure. Between 1982 and 1989, it had been just Tim and the branch managers, but since the acquisition of Sheratt & Hughes, although he continued to be both chairman and chief executive, a proper structure started to develop. More managing was being done through the board, although decision-making was still highly devolved.

Stage three: an observer

In 1993, Alan Giles came in to run Waterstone's from WHSmith, and in the succeeding five years built the profits from £10 million to £23 million, and the turnover from £130 million to £190 million.

During this period Tim turned his creative talents in a different direction, and began to write novels, with the first of three, *Lilley and Chase* (Hodder Headline), being published in 1994, which was followed by two more in two years.

But he found it hard to keep away from innovation in retailing. In 1997, inspired by the challenges of shopping with the two young daughters of his third marriage, he launched another new retail concept, Daisy & Tom, with its first branch in the King's Road. Daisy & Tom offers parents the benefit of convenience by bringing together a range of children's shops under one roof – books, toys, clothes, shoes and so on. To the children, it offers attractions such as a soda fountain, puppets and a carousel to provide an element of fun and fantasy.

But despite the distractions of what became two Daisy & Tom stores, despite the financial benefits of selling out, and despite the alternative outlet of his writing, Tim could not conceal the loss he felt at leaving Waterstone's: 'I just hated not having it. I got to the stage when I couldn't walk down the high street and see a Waterstone's without turning away. I loathed not having it.'

At one level he felt unfulfilled – that there was a lot that he had wanted to do with the business that now was not going to happen.

At another level he identified so closely with Waterstone's, and not just because it bore his name, that after he left he felt a sense of hurt, of having hurt it and himself by abandoning it.

Stage four: the buy-back

In 1997 WHSmith ran into some very public performance and succession problems. After allowing for reorganisation costs, they posted the first loss for 204 years, and that year Bill Cockburn, recently appointed chief executive from outside, resigned after only 18 months. Tim took the opportunity to put together what was described as an audacious, highly leveraged bid of £1.17 billion for the whole of the group.

His interest was not just in regaining the bookselling activities, but in turning round the WHSmith shops as well. He told a journalist at the time: 'I do know exactly what to do. I would chuck out the music, the videos, the awful Coke machines. I am completely passionate about doing a Waterstone's for the mid-market. I can't bear to watch it being run so incompetently. We would also have super stationery, absolutely beautiful stuff, and we would sell every newspaper and magazine.' By which he meant all the foreign language newspapers, minority periodicals, and every computer magazine. In other words, as authoritative a range in stationery and newspapers as Waterstone's carries in books. And he talked of raising the quality of the staff, with more graduates and more incentives.

Although WHSmith rejected this vision, and with it the offer of salvation, for Tim the experience was great fun: 'The run at Smiths was the funniest thing I have ever, ever been in. They made the terrible error of getting their press people to throw mud at me personally. The press did it for one day, but then we had a ball for three weeks returning it at Smiths. Effectively, they capitulated because of the pressure that we put on them through the press each day. Their advisers got the board together and said, "You'll have to do something, we can't hold this", so they just sprung out Waterstone's.'

For Tim that was a great moment: 'It feels as if my whole life has been a soap opera for the last 18 years, and that was just another extraordinary twist. When they said they would sell Waterstone's, it was about 6.45 a.m. and I was in my pyjamas. It was a great, great moment.'

At the time, he acknowledged the emotional significance: 'I am absolutely totally thrilled about this. Waterstone's is so much part of my heart that I am delighted to own it again.' However, in retrospect, he feels that the episode may have encouraged his reputation for ruthlessness: 'When you sell to somebody you are supposed to tiptoe away and fish for

the rest of your life. But I didn't. I hated them having it, and I was determined to get it back again. But we paid a very good price for it. Smiths did
very well with Waterstone's.'

The price that WHSmith got for the then 104 branches of Waterstone's was
£300 million. They were sold to a joint venture, HMV Media, which Tim
created with EMI and a venture capitalist, Advent International, to which
EMI sold its HMV, Dillons and Hatchards stores for up to £800 million.

Although Tim may have been delighted to be reunited with his great
love, he later found that the very fact that he had made a bid for WHSmith
laid to rest some important ghosts for him from years before: 'For 15 years
after I was fired by Smiths, I used to dream about them. Until I made a
hostile run at them, then all that stopped.'

Stage five: the story continues

Five years on, Waterstone's was still very much the company that Tim had
left in 1993: 'Alan Giles was sensible enough to leave the company very
much in the same style, although it has got to have been completely
against his instincts to do so. He brought in better systems and more
orthodox management techniques, but the Waterstone's we got back was
very, very similar to the one in 1993 – same people, same faces. It was
really a nice experience.'

But all did not continue that way. The integration of Waterstone's and
Dillons was painful, with costly delays in making decisions over whether to
run with one brand or two, and with greater centralisation under new operational management, which threatened to change the traditional culture.

A publicly reported drop in staff morale at the changes prompted specula-
tion at the end of 1999 that yet another twist in the story would result in Tim
making another buy-back of Waterstone's – this time from HMV Media.

Certainly Tim found being non-executive chairman at this time very
difficult emotionally: 'If I could, I would just fold my arms at this point
and say "Too late, don't worry about it", but I can't, I am too close to it. I
don't mind other people running Waterstone's, but in my lifetime it's not
going to be allowed to change. It is not going to be allowed to slip backwards into being an ordinary retailer. It should have 40 per cent of the
market, not 22 per cent.'

Overview

Because of the poetic twists and turns of the Waterstone story, and because, despite his modesty and diffidence, Tim makes 'good copy', he has frequently been profiled in the press. Maybe it is because he has defied stereotypes by having been both a businessman and a novelist; and traditional norms by having been married three times, and having eight children. Or, maybe it is because he is, as one journalist wrote: 'outspoken and often emotional', and therefore makes the interviewer's job easier.

Those who have interviewed him have used a variety of techniques to try to distil his essence. One such 'man of contrasts' approach was headlined as 'A battle of heart and head', as though the two were in conflict, and the heart out of place in business. Certainly in Tim's business life the heart appears to have been central in a number of ways.

He is strong on aspiration – one of his favourite quotations is from Goethe: 'Whatever you can do, or dream that you can do, begin it.' And on making a difference – there is something of a moral fervour in the way he talks of the impact that Waterstone's has had in saving the British book trade, and of the importance to the country of book retailing and publishing.

And then there is the creativity. Rather than see himself categorised as an entrepreneur, despite having at an early age reputedly sold his sweet ration to the bus queue in the village, Tim prefers the label of a creative who has turned some of his ideas into businesses.

He says: 'I'm a creative, wild and somewhat hyperactive person.' Although retail, for Tim, is about creative vision, not about detail. That's for others to worry about.

Certainly the ability to access his non-rational strengths, and to innovate, is evident in his empathy with what customers really want in terms of the retail experience – with what they want it to *feel* like to shop in a really 'browseable' bookshop, or in an exciting store for children.

This ability to empathise is not that far removed from that of intuition, which Tim also maintains is one of his strong suits: 'I'm very intuitive', he says, defending against accusations of favouritism on the basis that he's generally right.

He is able not just to access how he feels, but to harness those feelings and the energy they create. This is most noticeable in the way his anger against WHSmith drove him, from the white heat of the start-up through the twists and turns of the later parts of the story. This is fuelled partly by getting fired, but it combines explosively with another of his passions, class.

'I'm obsessed with class,' he says. This is not just because the brewers and the WHSmith of his early career were patronising, but because their system was unfair, unmeritocratic. An element of moral outrage creeps in.

Although anger can be harnessed, it cannot always be controlled, and it can manifest itself in impatience. When asked by a journalist whether there was any connection between his marriages and his career, and specifically whether potential investors should back a man who has been married three times, on the basis that he may be lacking in commitment, he replied: 'I think there is an impatience with personal situations that fail. There is also an impatience with business situations that fail. I think that's your connection if there is one.'

Tim is both open to his feelings and open about his feelings, which strengthens his ability to connect with others, and to lead and inspire them. He is able to be himself in business in a way that many people who are stifled by the conformity of hierarchies feel unable to be. There is little difference between the values of Waterstone the man and Waterstone's the business.

However, this openness can be painful: 'I'm pretty thin-skinned, and I absolutely loathe criticism', he says. This sensitivity can take refuge in self-deprecation, or what appears to be self-deprecation. At one time he took pleasure in repeating a journalist's remark that he was boring – 'about as interesting as meeting a lock-keeper on a disused canal'.

The openness can reveal a familiarity with the darker side of human nature. His description of an entrepreneur is someone who is bossy, egotistical, demanding, pig-headed, ignorant and aggressive: 'They are very bad at working for other people... entrepreneurs have huge egos... you would think they are possessed... the entrepreneur is naturally aggressive.'

Tim also shares his familiarity with suffering. He has had direct experience of periods of depression in his earlier life, and the two divorces have left their share of pain. In a *Sunday Times* article in the Relative Values series, he said of the end of his first marriage: 'Being separated from three children was unbelievably painful. I will always remember my father driving Richard and his younger brother away to take them back to my separated wife, and Richard peering out of the back window at me. It was the most painful experience of my life.' Looking back, he says: 'The major thing I really wished had happened in my life was a completely solid domestic background.'

Some of this pain may be worked out in his own writing. In his first novel, *Lilley and Chase*, there is a misunderstood bookseller called Tom Waterwell, and a chapter about a father telling his daughter that he is leaving that is so autobiographical that Tim says he can't read it without crying.

But some of it may also be mirrored in the continuing relationship with that other creation, called Waterstone's. That is certainly a relationship in which Tim does leave, but finds it impossible to let go, and returns.

So, with such a powerful connection between self and business, how does Tim maintain any sort of balance in his life? Clearly his family plays a major role. He describes his third wife, Rosie, a television director, as 'a hugely stabilising influence on me'. And he is fortunate enough to still have two young daughters and deliberately makes time each day to play an active role in their lives. He hates working in the evening, and switches off by being with his family, and by spending time on his own writing.

He has also learned to conserve his own emotional energy: 'I'm a lot wiser in personal relations. I keep out of quarrels – the personal name-calling. It's not that I don't care. I don't get emotionally involved, it's so counter-productive.'

And he has grown more self-aware in terms of what causes him stress: 'What I teach my children is to face up to problems. It removes the stress. It's the unresolved problems that wear you down.'

9 Dr Ashok Ganguly

Introduction

This chapter is somewhat different to the others in that it focuses on an individual and his impact in a number of environments. It is not the story of a business transformation in the same way as a number of the others have been, but rather it talks about the transformational impact of the individual and his work with an organisation within the context of a broader environment. The individual is Dr Ashok Ganguly.

Dr Ganguly has been included in this book for a number of reasons:

- He is a highly successful and professional businessman who has delivered results for a range of stakeholders in a number of diverse businesses; most notably Hindustan Lever, the Indian subsidiary of Unilever, where he worked from 1962–90 holding the post of chairman India from 1980 to 1990. During this period he was pivotal in many crucial and successful changes to the business as measured from the commercial perspective. However, equally impactful and possibly more significant was his role in transforming a number of other dimensions – some internal (the relationship between R&D and business processes); and others external (the business and the external environment; the business and its relationship to broader society; business and education; and business and government).

- He is an acknowledged expert in the field of science and technology and his views on how to improve the effectiveness of the research and development function are held in high regard around the world.

- His ability and track record in demonstrating effective management across a number of different cultural environments both geographic (India, USA and Europe) and functional (research, manufacturing and general management).

■ His ability to bridge the gap between a number of different worlds previously separated by somewhat fuzzy boundaries, for example business and politics and R&D and commercial.

■ His role as a champion for India.

For all these reasons, this chapter is therefore not so much the story of a single transformation and more the story of the impact of an individual with a particular set of characteristics on others, both individuals and organisations, around him and, of course, the impact this had on him.

Biodata

Dr Ganguly is the chairman of ICI India Ltd and a non-executive member of the boards of British Airways, ICICI, Mahindra & Mahindra, ICICI Knowledge Park Ltd and WIPRO Ltd. He is also a member of the government's Technology Board. In addition, he heads his own company, Technology Network (India) Pvt Ltd, dedicated to industrial R&D, strategy and supply chain management and high technology partnerships between foreign and Indian SMEs.

Dr Ganguly's principal professional career spanned 35 years with Unilever. He was the chairman of Hindustan Lever Ltd from 1980–90 and a member of Unilever's main board from 1990–97, responsible for worldwide research and technology.

He was selected as India's Businessman of the Year in 1986. In 1987, the President of India conferred upon him the Padma Bhushan, one of India's highest honours, for his contribution to public service. In May 1991, he was elected a Fellow of the Royal Society of Chemistry, and in 1995 he was awarded an Honorary Fellowship in the Jawaharla Nehru Centre for Advanced Scientific Research. In 1996, Dr Ganguly was conferred the title of Honorary Professor by the Chinese Academy of Sciences in Shanghai. The University of Illinois selected Dr Ganguly as their 'Outstanding Alumni' in 1997.

Dr Ganguly has several publications to his credit on the topics of management, science and contemporary issues. He authored a book *Industry and Liberalisation* in 1994, published by Allied Publishers Ltd, and has co-authored another, entitled *Strategic Manufacturing for Competitive Advantage* published in 1998 by Oxford & IBH Publishing Co Pvt Ltd.

Dr Ganguly's latest book, entitled *Business-driven Research and Development – Managing Knowledge to Create Wealth,* was published by Macmillan UK in June 1998.

Over the years Dr Ganguly has been involved with many and diverse professional and national organisations in Europe and in India.

Background and career path

Dr Ganguly's grandparents were a land-owning family from Bangladesh. His father worked as an engineer and spent all of his life in Bombay. He was a middle-class professional without land. His lifestyle, although modest, was very comfortable and family life was happy and relaxed. Dr Ganguly was the younger of two children, having an older sister. He describes his parents as being very supportive, encouraging the children without placing undue expectations on them. This built within the children a sense of confidence and developed a balance within which both achievement and minor failure could be met with a sense of equanimity. There was neither undue celebration of success nor unnecessary focus on underachievement, but rather an encouragement to do one's best and focus both on one's talents and being true to oneself.

Throughout most of his early education, Ashok Ganguly was, by his own admission, an average student. This, however, changed dramatically at 16 and continued on through his university career. Commenting on this change, Ashok says 'there was a staggering difference in the quality of teachers at the run-of-the-mill school I attended, compared to the commitment and passion of the college lecturers and professors I encountered at Bombay University – they inspired me. Also, I came to realise my scholastic abilities over the course of the four years and ended up with scholarships, prizes and a rank in my graduating year – something defiantly worth having!'

He suddenly discovered in chemistry, through some inspired teaching, a passion which captivated and motivated him. He became an outstanding student, taking a top honours degree in chemistry at Bombay University. He and his parents were delighted and he went off to continue his studies in the USA with a major scholarship. He took a Master's and a PhD at the University of Illinois. Having completed his education and having had a thoroughly enjoyable and successful time in the USA, he returned to India for a well-earned vacation with the intention of deciding what to do next.

One of the key factors in my decision not to return to a teaching and research career in the USA was a realisation of how my parents had aged during the six years I had been away from home – during this time my father had suffered and recovered from a fairly serious heart problem.

The decision as to what to do next was also helped, in a way, by a Government of India scheme, inspired by Nehru, that any individual, returning to India after postgraduate studies abroad who did not have a job, became entitled to a monthly stipend and a choice of working in any state institution of their choice until they were able to secure a more permanent and suitable position commensurate with their qualifications.

These were both factors, but overall the challenge of having the opportunity to be in the mainstream of developments in my own country was extremely attractive and appealing!

Thus, somewhat to his own surprise he decided to remain in India and make his career and life there. The country had a number of major economic issues, a significant proportion of its population was still extremely poor, business was still highly regulated and the commercial environment was not viewed as a major world player. However, Ashok felt a strong desire to be part of the growing number of internationally educated young who were excited by the challenges facing the country after independence and who were committed to making a difference and playing a role in the creation of a new India.

But after a few months as a government-sponsored researcher, Ashok came to the conclusion that his fundamental scientific interest could only be undertaken in the USA. If he were to remain and work in India in the long term, he would have to explore broader goals and avenues via the professionally managed private sector industries of India. After some searching, he joined Unilever's Indian subsidiary, Hindustan Lever, as part of their graduate trainee scheme and stayed with them for the next 28 years, a period he describes fondly as 'a continuous chain of excitement'. He spent significant periods of his career in Holland, the USA and India. From 1962 to 1970, he spent his time in the research function, starting out as an assistant research scientist. In addition to his scientific know-how and education, he brought a number of other attributes, namely, 'energy, enthusiasm, a passion for making a difference and people skills'. During this period, he observed continually and learnt an immense amount from the Unilever approach, taking on board a number of values which stayed with him throughout his career and fundamentally shaped his approach to leadership; he absolutely believed in the value of operating a meritocracy and admired the Unilever ability to 'take ordinary people and enable and equip them to perform extraordinarily'.

India has always had more bright and capable people compared to the opportunities available. And in spite of the large number of scientists and engineers emigrating to the USA every year – the brain drain – local companies still had an excellent pool of talent to choose from. Hindustan Lever was, and still is, considered the most attractive employer among the multinationals. It was considered the best profes- sionally managed company, where individual skill and competency were the only determinants in defining career progression.

Ashok thrived in this environment. The self-confidence he had gained as an undergraduate had been reinforced and blossomed under his PhD mentor in America. Ashok recalls:

When I started my research work, my first set of experiments produced incorrect results compared to those published in the literature. During a six-month period, I undertook this experiment several times without success. Each failure was followed by a discussion with my research guide. And every time he listened patiently and then we would briefly discuss what I would do next. As a graduate student, I was required to attend lectures during the day, so long research experiments had to be undertaken at night. One night I discovered what I had been doing incorrectly and went on to produce, confirm and reconfirm the right results. I was stunned by the foolishness of the error but elated to have solved the problem myself! I was intrigued as to why my professor had not pointed out this simple mistake, and when I asked him next morning he replied 'If I had told you what to do, how would you have ever found out for yourself?' What a wonderful lesson!

There was a second occasion when Ashok and his professor were trying to uncover the possible structure of a molecule. This had involved several experiments, the accumulation of piles of data leading to the development of a hypothesis. Ashok had returned home from the laboratory fairly late on a bleak Midwestern winter's evening. While thumbing through the data over and over again he lapsed into a tired sleep – when he woke up it was 3 a.m. In his mind he had the beginnings of the possible structure of the new molecule. He rushed back to the laboratory and began preparing notes on his ideas ready for discussion with his professor. They eventually solved the mystery. The lesson he took away from this was that: 'you have to develop the ability to visualise ideas and just let them tumble around in your mind – this is the way to find the undiscovered.' It is a motto he kept with him for the rest of his career.

He had a thoroughly enjoyable time with Hindustan Lever in India and a particularly successful research sojourn in Holland. He discovered in himself a strong and sought-after ability to motivate others, encouraging both himself and them to question the status quo and change the rules when necessary. In particular, his impact on the Dutch research function was strong, being described by those who worked with him at the time as 'inspirational – a period of personal satisfaction and success which many have never been able to recapture'.

Indeed his time in Holland was so successful that Unilever were very keen for him to stay in Europe. He had identified as a key weakness the lack of connection between R&D and the marketplace and recognised that a much more profound understanding of consumers and customers together with a radical change in the management of R&D was necessary to make it an unambiguous and business relevant process. He recognised the need to get scientists to understand business without losing their natural curiosity. Building this connection between science and business was something he continued to work on throughout his career. Often he encountered entrenched views and many cases of 'us versus them'. Despite the frustrations of attempting to overcome these barriers, he never lost his ability to remain positive and focused on the future. Yet he often found himself frustrated by 'the utter arrogance and remoteness from the realities of the marketplace of individual scientists'.

Return to India

Despite an enormously successful European stay, Dr Ganguly says, 'it was a non-decision to go back. It just felt right!' Ashok had come to the conclusion that, while industry was not the platform for undertaking the type of fundamental research he was interested in, there was for him a huge attraction in the other areas of management. While different, they represented a complex and difficult challenge – one he was prepared to have a go at.

Together with his wife Connie, he weighed up the pros and cons of a very comfortable life in Holland, with the attraction of leading and managing significant research in industry, against a return to India. In the end the decision to return was not at all difficult: 'I was attracted by the excitement of working in Hindustan Lever despite the uncertainty of what the future may hold.'

Having made the decision, they quickly settled down in Bombay and, three months after returning to India, the chairman called Ashok telling him he was to be given an opportunity to broaden his area of expertise – in short he was offered an opportunity to move to manufacturing. Reflecting back on the call, Ashok says:

I was promised nothing; it was a sink or swim opportunity, yet I really did not hesitate for long. I made the decision and I left research and moved into manufacturing. While the period in research was intellectually an extremely satisfying one and a wonderful way to start a career with Hindustan Lever, my real grounding in management began with this move and grew as I began to find my feet on the shopfloors of the factories in Bombay and Calcutta.

Again it was not the most risk-averse decision that Ashok could have taken, yet he decided that the risk was worth the potential it offered him for the future. Still it was not without some trepidation that he made the move:

Any young Unilever manager will understand the feeling of having to almost restart a career after eight years in the company and at a couple of classes lower, with no promise of what the future might hold – and I was not that young either! One may empathise with this momentary unease that went through my mind on being appointed as the soap packing manager in a Bombay factory and being put in charge of almost 400 people!

However, he did indeed swim. From 1970 to 1976, he gained experience of all aspects of the shopfloor to become the most senior technical general manager in the business. Every four to six months he was offered and took a larger job. He took an uncomplicated and natural approach to all his dealings on the shopfloor, and quickly won the trust of the large workforce and their shop stewards. He also quickly discovered that, with the help of those at the sharp end, most manufacturing problems were solvable by hypothesis development and logical analysis. These approaches were reinforced across multiple assignments, and his confidence in both his management philosophy and his leadership approach grew.

He believes that a large part of this phenomenal progression was also, to some extent, due to luck; being in the right place at the right time and being given the right breaks.

Yet he clearly performed way above expectations and delivered huge success.

These are years of very fond memories, particularly of those who readily shared their own years of experience to help me through my initial, hesitant days in dealing with a whole set of strange problems such as unprocessable soap and veteran union leaders. I learned a great deal from a number of experienced workmen, supervisors and trade union leaders on how to seek solutions to what at times appeared to be intractable problems.

During this period he was identified as the potential future chairman and put on a fast track development programme. 'I was gaining in confidence in spades and totally immersed in my work.'

Ashok's work day spanned an average of 12–16 hours a day, sometimes longer. Sundays and short breaks were spent with his wife and two young daughters. Family life in India was made up of simple pleasures; a car ride to the seaside, a short vacation to see the sand dunes of Rajasthan. But most of his life revolved around work, work and more work. Recollecting this period he says, 'Connie was a great support through all of this work and the principal inspiration throughout my career. In retrospect I may have been occasionally somewhat selfish.'

Eventually, in 1977, he was appointed to the board of Hindustan Lever. Dr Ganguly says:

Everything that happened up to then was a surprise. I had not planned my career; I just did what felt right and made decisions about the next move as they came along. Self-confidence, having fun and a concern for people as individuals is critical. Motivating yourself and others is the key to success.

I have never been anxious about what I am or where I am going – why should I be happy or miserable about others' success or failure? History does not excite me, what does is a focus on the future and what can be achieved. I have always been a firm believer, and hopefully I have demonstrated, that if you are more interested in building others than in building yourself, you will get far more performance and deliver better results! Focusing on one's own future is a barrier to achievement.

Leadership style

On talking to Dr Ganguly about how this meteoric rise impacted on him personally, he clearly identified 'the discipline is to distinguish between your role as a family member and that as a professional manager and behaving accordingly' as being the key.

> The ability to distinguish between one's personal life and professional role is important to sustain balance in society.

> Usually individuals who have a happy family upbringing develop the trait of self-esteem which has very little to do with their professional activities and achievements. In my experience, individuals who lack this sense of self-esteem use their professional achievements as a surrogate. I strongly believe that mixing personal and professional roles detracts from objectivity and hampers one's ability to be a leader.

Yet a number of his personal characteristics were clearly employed in both arenas, namely, excitement, curiosity, commitment, a positive and optimistic outlook and an impatience with dogma. When these characteristics combined with his global perspective, his absolute belief in meritocracy and his future focus, it is not difficult to understand how he impacted on those around him.

Despite the enormous pressures and challenges he faced during this period, his inclination to see the constraints not as a threat but as an opportunity gave him a unique leadership style.

> It is not those with personal charisma and performance alone who emerge as leaders. It is those who enable individuals, people and nations to gain the self-confidence to achieve by, their individual and collective efforts, social and economic objectives – they are the real leaders of the future.

He faced major challenges from disruptive trade unions, a phenomenon that was sweeping India throughout the 1970s and 80s. Hindustan Lever's biggest factory in Bombay employed more than 4000 workers and was threatened with disruption and potential closure by the actions of its militant trade union leader. This obviously caused significant concern to Ashok and his team. After much heartache and at not inconsiderable risk, Ashok planned and implemented a strategic plan to counter the threat by the development of a number of fallback options of dispersing manufacturing across the country. This bold move not only overcame the threat but also, even more significantly, brought to an end the disruptive activities of the trade union leader – something other companies had failed to do.

It was also during this period that Hindustan Lever faced a severe challenge from low-cost producers competing on a number of its premium products. The story of how the challenge was successfully tackled and Dr Ganguly's role in this is now an important Unilever case study, used on its senior management training courses. The low-cost business model is now Unilever best practice around the world.

Another landmark was Hindustan Lever's success in persuading the government to allow Unilever to retain majority shareholding in India. This was against a context of draconian policies against multinationals which had forced such organisations as Coca-Cola and IBM to discontinue business in India, and others such as Philips and Nestlé to become minority shareholders in their Indian subsidiaries.

When asked how those who worked with him during this period would have described him he says 'tough, stern and demanding, but fair and supportive'. While this may be an accurate description of the standards he expected and the excellence he sought, one suspects that it fails to capture his charisma and the impact of his personal style and enthusiasm on others.

From strength to strength

In 1980 having completed the senior Sloan programme at MIT, he was invited to lunch by the chairman in London and appointed as chairman India. This coincided with the Congress Party. under Indira Gandhi, being returned to power. Industrial policy in India made major strides forward and the term 'liberalisation' was first coined, heralding a shift in the relationship between government and commerce. Although this did not result in any tangible benefits for a long time, there was a sense of anticipation that India's industrial and economic policies were about to undergo profound change. In reflecting on this, Dr Ganguly says:

Industry had the potential to be one of the most potent unifying economic forces in modern India. It had to be transformed into an effective weapon to counter the fissiparous tendencies that sought to destabilise the nation and the ideals we cherished.

Thus he relished the opportunity to play a role in strengthening the position of industry.

During the following decade, Dr Ganguly led Hindustan Lever at the forefront of delivering the transformation of this relationship. The period 1980 to 1990 was a combination of personal success and satisfying corporate performance. He was leading the Indian arm of a large and prominent multinational which continued to deliver beneficial results for its shareholders, while simultaneously delivering a huge and sustainable impact for its broader stakeholders, particularly those who worked for the organisation throughout India. It was truly a period that made a difference. Dr Ganguly, reflecting on this period, says:

I consider my 10 years as the chairman of Hindustan Lever the most happy, fulfilling and satisfying, not primarily because of what may have been achieved, but because I was responsible for a corporation which received social, commercial and public acclaim, due entirely to the collective effort of the vast majority of employees in the company. I cherish the experience of helping to strengthen an environment in Hindustan Lever that enabled people to work as individuals and teams with dignity and commitment. When you get a group of highly intelligent, well-trained and committed people, they will give their best if you create conditions which enable them to do so.

When asked about any key lessons he took away from this period, Dr Ganguly said:

It was much, much later that I realised that leaders who are able to combine passion, energy and intellect readily inspire other individuals and groups in ways that are difficult to describe and therefore to teach to others.

During this period, the Hindustan Lever business achieved some notable successes. Ten new factories were built – an unprecedented number. The Bombay factory was reorganised to enable it to be managed outside the shadow of militant trade unions. This reorganisation heralded a major shift in labour–management relationships. Technology breakthroughs were also made, particularly in soap chemistry and technology, which went on to become a powerful plank of the Indian business's cost, quality and competitive strategy.

In addition to leading the internal performance of Hindustan Lever, Dr Ganguly was pioneering the development of a close, professional relationship with the government. It was an emerging role in the new India and required the balancing of the interests of shareholders and the company against those of the nation and the people. It required great delicacy and carried an awesome 'sense of responsibility'. Often during this period, Dr Ganguly came under pressure from the different constituencies he was trying to balance.

Her own bodyguards had assassinated Indira Gandhi in October 1984. Rajiv Gandhi won a resounding victory in the ensuing elections and was elected Prime Minister in January 1985.

I had known Rajiv earlier and he wanted me to assist in areas concerning industry, science and technology. In 1985, I was appointed as a member of his Science Advisory Council and from 1985 to 1990 spent considerable time assisting the government in areas ranging from exports to energy conservation.

Some of my colleagues at the time may have felt I was getting too close to the government for comfort. I tried to explain to some of them, as I had indeed told most people I knew well in the government, that one did not run a corporation like Hindustan Lever by befriending people in the right places or by seeking favours. Rather, one participates in public affairs and government committees in order to establish a more sustainable understanding of each other's point of view. To criticise something one must be on the inside.

The wisdom of the role played by Hindustan Lever in the public arena became apparent with the passage of time. Symbolically, it was acclaimed by rewards and recognition. Ashok Ganguly was chosen as India's 'Businessman of the Year' in 1986 and the President of India conferred upon him the Padma Bhushan. This is one of the nation's highest honours and had never before been conferred on a multinational chairman, and rarely even on an Indian business leader.

Despite sometimes feeling as if he was caught in the middle of a number of conflicting priorities, Dr Ganguly continued to rely on his own personal resources and to use his leadership skills in trying to achieve progress for all involved.

As time went by, it became apparent to me that when you are able to attract, inspire and delegate wisely to competent colleagues, it releases time to allow you to focus energy on thinking about the broader vision.

His approach to what he describes as 'human relations dynamics' was not dissimilar to his approach as a research scientist, where he employed a hypothesis-driven philosophy to try to deliver progress. His approach to business remained a very human one; he sees business not in technical, but in human, terms:

> The nature of human relationships and interactions determines the quality, productivity and flow of knowledge across vast networks and it is this which ultimately determines the innovation and wealth-creating ability of most businesses.

During this period as chairman, Dr Ganguly had an increasingly high profile. He was the visible face of a company that represented excellence and therefore his views and opinions were actively sought out across a number of forums. In addition to his work of chairing Hindustan Lever, he served on a number of important decision-making bodies. His work as a member of the Science Advisory Council was extremely rewarding and, and as a representative on the board of Research Councils, where he was the only industrial member, he was able to link government concerns closely with the Lever board. Dr Ganguly recalls the years of 1980–90 with great excitement.

> The period of 1980–90 was a watershed decade, in that India decided to break away from the shackles of low growth, poverty and illiteracy by freeing the productive energies and intellect of its people. Yet it has taken until now for the first fruits of this change to become evident.

His surprise at having achieved the status of chairman was supplemented by the sense of privilege and excitement he now felt at being involved in managing things on a broader perspective. Highlights he mentions from this period involved his meetings and discussions with world figures, notably President Gorbachev of Russia who was preaching glasnost and perestroika, President Laurent Fabius, President Mitterand, Margaret Thatcher, Queen Elizabeth, Queen Juliana and Prince Klaus of the Netherlands, to name but a few, and his first association with Mother Teresa since 1973, an experience which he 'greatly cherished'.

Despite his high profile and sought-after status, he never forgot that he was a representative of an organisation and he 'derived strength from knowing my own limitations and reminding myself everyday that all the achievements were made possible by a dedicated group of employees at Hindustan Lever'. He had set himself the personal target of remaining as chairman for no more than ten years.

As this period came to an end, he considered his options as to what to do next.

One of my predecessors had made a wise comment which had stuck in my mind. He believed one should stay as leader of a business for at least five years. This gives accountability in facing one's own mistakes. And never longer than ten years, when one tends to block the growth of people and ideas.

As a result of his exposure to government and his commitment to playing a role in delivering the new India, inevitably he considered shifting the focus of his career to the political arena. By now he had developed a close and trusting personal relationship with Rajiv Gandhi, whom he admired hugely and who was actively pressing him to stand for a parliamentary seat.

He found much in common with Gandhi's approach to the future and to change, being inspired by the following quote:

India is an old country, but a young nation; and like the young everywhere we are impatient. I am young, and I too have a dream. I dream of an India strong, independent and self-reliant and in the front rank of the nations of the world in the service of mankind. I am committed to realising this dream through dedication, hard work and the collective determination of our people. We will welcome all the co-operation we can get.

When, in 1991, the elections were declared, he was finally persuaded by Gandhi to come for a strategy discussion at the end of May. In his own mind, having agreed to the meeting, he had emotionally committed to such a move but, when Gandhi was killed that month, it was an end of a dream and an experience which he found 'personally devastating' and which fundamentally changed his view as to his own future.

I have not yet come to a conclusion whether I was attracted to politics because of Rajiv Gandhi's leadership and friendship or whether I had a natural inclination. It is too early for me to know conclusively, but I feel it was most likely a little of both. It took me a long, long time to recover from the tragedy of Rajiv's assassination. I now spend more time in India and less in England. I enjoy the orderliness of life in Europe and the space for thought that it provides me, but I also feel the old urge of wanting to do something more substantive in the Indian landscape. I am passionate about what the new knowledge revolution can do to improve the lot of the poor. Information technology and genomics are the two pillars of the knowledge revolution and I have set up my own company to help to deliver some of the benefits that knowledge can bring. I believe helping people to create wealth should be at the heart of public service in a 21st-century India.

As a direct consequence of Gandhi's assassination, he decided not to pursue a political career. Instead he remained in the world of international business.

10 Robin Buchanan and
Orit Gadeish

This chapter is also about leaders and transformation. It is, however, different from our earlier stories in that it focuses on a business transformation and the subsequent rebuilding of a major organisation, told from the perspective of two individuals who were part of the 60-strong leadership team involved in this change. The transformation itself is somewhat unusual in that, unlike, and contrary to, much of what our own consulting experience has shown us, it was not driven by a single leader but rather by a leadership team of very different sorts of people in multiple locations around the world – indeed the transformation was highly significant in confirming the culture of the team and cementing the individuals together in such a way that, ten years later, very nearly all of the players are still with the business today.

Business background

Bain and Company is one of the world's foremost management consultancies. It advises a significant number of the world's top CEOs and their organisations and is one of the top three consultancy destinations to which many of the best and brightest graduates from the elite business schools aspire. It employs 3000 consultants and has 26 offices around the world (it had six in 1989). It has a client retention rate of 85 per cent which is one of the highest in the industry, and a client satisfaction rating which is second to none. Its reputation is based on the firm's ability to deliver significant benefits to its clients through analytical rigour, intellectual integrity and a commitment to deliverable implementation. It has a history of innovation, many of these having become benchmarks for the consulting industry as a whole.

William (Bill) Bain, who had begun his consulting career only six years earlier, established Bain and Company in 1973. He had quickly become disillusioned with the short-term, transactional nature of much of the consulting he had been involved in, and set up Bain and Company to be different, with a commitment to establishing long-term relationships with clients based on the delivery of measurable results. The new business, with its mix of data-driven challenge and practical implementation planning, quickly had impact with clients and soon enjoyed rapid growth and early success. A number of, at the time unique, characteristics were instrumental in fuelling the growth, and later had significant implications for the business when it hit difficulties.

Bill Bain strongly believed in integrity and trust and committed to his clients that the consultancy would only work for one company in any given competitive battle at any one time. He placed huge emphasis on confidentiality and went to unusual lengths to safeguard the identity of his clients and the nature of the work that Bain was undertaking with them. He passionately believed that the work done by his organisation would speak for itself and therefore shunned any kind of formal marketing, relying instead on word of mouth recommendation from client to client. He recruited from among the brightest graduates of the top business schools and the organisation quickly took on a strong and distinctive culture that was somewhat exclusive to those outside. This all contributed to a mystique which allowed myths to grow up around the business.

For more than a decade, the business enjoyed phenomenal success and enviable growth. In the 1970s and 80s, Bain's growth rate massively outperformed the 15 per cent annual average growth rate for consulting firms by a large margin. Then two events happened in quick succession, which were to put not just this success but the entire future of the business in jeopardy. In the UK, the Guinness scandal hit the headlines. Oliver Roux, one of Bain's partners, had been seconded to Guinness as its financial director. Thus, the name of Bain became widely known and, although later officially exonerated by the DTI, the negative publicity, in the absence of any counterbalancing press, damaged the company's reputation.

At around the same time, after more than a decade of meteoric growth, Bill Bain and the other seven founding partners decided the time was right to reap the rewards of their labours. In 1985 and 1986, in two separate transactions, the eight partners (including the seven founding partners) sold 30 per cent of the company to create an ESOP (Employee Stock Ownership Plan). The valuation of the business, which was to prove somewhat controversial, was based on the historical growth rate with extrapolation thereof into the future. The founding partners received a total of approximately $200 million which the company had to borrow, leaving the firm with around $25 million in interest payments, due each year, to be paid out of the future revenues of the firm.

These interest rates were to prove crippling as the business turned down. The consulting industry as a whole took a downturn after the boom of the 1980s, as the worldwide recession took hold. At Bain, revenues fell off and the business found itself with a cashflow problem which, unless solved quickly, could drive the business to bankruptcy. Business floundered as the recession and the Gulf War took their toll. In 1988, as interest payments continued to grow significantly, Bain laid off 10 per cent of its US consultants, with a further 300 being laid off soon afterwards. Most of these consultants were higher-level, long-time employees and represented the first lay-offs in the firm's history. Morale plummeted; internally, it was felt to be 'a breach of the social contract'. The problems peaked in 1990/1991 when the business was faced with two major problems; a financial situation which impacted the business globally and which threatened the very survival of the business, and a London operation close to collapse, as the Guinness scandal continued to significantly damage future prospects.

Consultancies are in many ways a unique type of business – full of high achievers, usually with accompanying high egos. They are usually relatively independent and have strong opinions of their own. They do not see themselves operating in hierarchies, but rather respond to a 'first among equals' approach. They are unlikely to respond to being told to do something, and would rather have the facts presented to them and be left to draw their own conclusions. Managing a group of consultants is often likened to 'herding cats'! Consultants, as a group of individuals, have to be led rather than managed.

The urgency of the financial situation was becoming critical, with a number of press articles, notably 'Physician, Heal Thyself' in *Forbes* and 'Did Greed Cripple Bain and Company' in the *Boston Globe*, continuing to create damage in the marketplace. Bill Bain, recognising the seriousness of the situation, eventually asked Mitt Romney, CEO of Bain Capital (itself one of the top three performing funds in the world), the consultancies' sister company, to take on the job of sorting out the financial recapitalisation of the business that was necessary to secure the future. It was a classic financial reengineering job, largely technical, aimed at stopping the bleeding. At the same time, the partners appointed a management committee of 15 partners to oversee the transformation.

Romney renegotiated Bain's position with the banks, the founding partners and other involved players in order to develop a more sustainable financial position. As one of the partners, Tom Tierney, then head of the Californian office who went on to become worldwide managing director of the firm, commented: 'We still owed a lot of money but at least we were solvent.' With the financial turnaround in hand, it was possible to turn the focus to other elements of the transformation.

In London, the situation was desperate – the Guinness scandal continued to impact heavily. Seventy per cent of revenue had been lost over the previous 12 months and the business was projected to lose 70 per cent of the remaining business over the next four months. Some key senior figures had left to form a breakaway business. The office was being led by an individual who proved to be the wrong man at the wrong time. Defections from the firm by managers and consultants were running at a rate of nearly 30 per cent a year. New clients were not being cultivated, old relationships were allowed to wither, partners were not working with each other and team spirit had evaporated. Dissatisfaction with the management style reached a peak in the summer of 1990, with five of London's twelve partners offering their resignation. Bill Bain met with the five partners, who included Robin Buchanan and Crawford Gillies (who is now the managing partner of the London office) in an effort to persuade them to reconsider their decision. Eventually it was agreed that the only outcome that could persuade them to reverse their resignations was if they had the opportunity to lead the London office and design a transformation plan for the British business. Bill Bain agreed to this if they could identify and agree among themselves and one other partner who was to lead the business forward.

The six partners spent a huge amount of time talking among themselves; they did not, until then, know each other well. But through the process of these discussions, they discovered a deep respect for each other's professionalism and a shared belief in the core values of the company, recognising that these values were what had initially attracted each of them to the firm and were values which resonated with their own personal value systems. Furthermore, each of them believed passionately in the intrinsic value of the firm's brand and the work that Bain delivered. They quickly recognised that two things were critical – a short-term plan for the office and leadership. Robin Buchanan was asked by the others to take on the leadership role. In reflecting back on this period Robin says:

Although there were stylistic differences among us, we quickly realised that we all cared about the same things and agreed unanimously on what things were important! In looking forward, we wanted to achieve the same things for the business and strongly felt that delivering outstanding results to clients absolutely described what we were trying to do.

We didn't have much information to go on, because none of us were privy to the financial records of the company. But we understood three basic things: what we really cared about; what our clients really cared about; and what we were really good at versus the competition. We knew what we stood for and we knew we had to refocus the business along these guiding principles.

Robin Buchanan – background and career path

Robin Buchanan is a highly sophisticated and experienced consultant. He is warm and approachable, listens carefully and is direct in his responses. He is clearly used to guiding conversations and is a skilful and articulate communicator. He is thoughtful and speaks with great affection of Stan Miranda, Crawford Gillies, Luc Luyten and his other colleagues in the partner group, and it is obvious that it is the people behind the roles that matter most to him.

He was described by Orit Gadeish as:

A brilliant consultant and a unique individual. He has a brilliant and incisive mind and is uniquely honest. As a friend and colleague, I value him highly. The best way of describing him is that he has 'flair'.

Born in 1952, Robin was the eldest of three children. His father was a Scot who, after being injured in the Second World War, came to London and had a highly successful career as a stockbroker. He had a strong influence on Robin, instilling in him a commitment to the motto 'meum dictum pactum' (my word is my bond) and a 'work hard, play hard' ethic. Robin says he inherited 'an entrepreneurial spirit, a terrible laugh and a very strong desire to tell the truth!' Robin's mother, too, was a major influence. She was also strongly entrepreneurial. Robin is extremely proud of her, describing her as 'very strong with extraordinary energy'. Her influence on him drove much of his passion, enthusiasm and energy.

Robin went to a Sussex boarding school at the age of eight, which he 'loved' and then on to Eton, with which he was less enamoured. He developed a somewhat rebellious streak, and this, combined with an unfortunately timed accident, meant that he did not gain a university place on leaving school. Instead, he worked his way through a number of unusual and rewarding roles, gaining exposure to a host of interesting business issues at a very early age, until he eventually ended up in the USA. He was persuaded to apply to Harvard Business School (something his father had also earlier advised), applied and became one of only three individuals who did not have an undergraduate degree ever to be accepted. At Harvard, he fell in love with the higher education he had never had before and absolutely revelled in the mixture of US enthusiasm and entrepreneurialism he encountered. He did a summer internship with McKinsey, and despite liking the people, he decided consulting was not for him. Instead, he joined American Express International Banking Corporation in order to pursue an interest in Third World economies. After a number of years working here with great success, he became disillusioned with the politics and he joined Bain in Boston in 1982. 'I loathe corporate politics and wanted something different.' At Bain, he quickly enjoyed huge success. One of his first assignments was in helping to set up the hugely successful sister company, Bain Capital. He soon worked his way up the management structure. However, in 1990, he became disillusioned with the style and values of the then head of the office. This led to his decision to quit which helped to crystallise the issues to be faced during the turnaround.

Turning round the London office

On 29 October 1990, it was announced to the London office that a new management team was in place, headed by Robin Buchanan as managing partner. The team immediately set about the task of transforming the business for the future. 'The night Crawford, Stan, Luc and I took over, our first job was to stop the bleeding,' said Buchanan.

> We had to make some critical and painful management and leadership choices; we had to ensure business success and we knew that we simply could not sustain the size of the office as it was. We had to cut costs and secure the balance sheet.

> Between 4 pm, when the memo was first read to the office, and 10 pm, the six members of the new management team met with every single staff member of the UK operation at various London hotels to reconsider and rationalise the business. At the time, London was responsible for the international business covering diverse geographies such as Italy, Australia and Canada. As a consequence, it carried an amount of corporate overhead. We had to cut back. We had to give to ourselves, and take, the advice we give to our clients; in short, we had to take some of our own medicine.

It was an enormously difficult process; we were dealing with lots of friends and people we cared a great deal about, as well as tackling some complicated legal issues. We were only able to give a half-hour maximum to each person and of course some people needed much more time than this. It was emotionally draining. We felt the huge responsibility we had to these people and had a deep desire to do things properly. We wanted to take care of individuals and recognised that the decisions we were taking would have a huge impact on their careers. These were horribly difficult decisions and the process has forever given me huge empathy with clients facing similar situations. By 10 o'clock that night, we had agreed the separation of 43 people from the office, including two partners – this represented a third of the entire consulting staff. Having been through the experience, I vowed never again to allow myself, or any business I was involved in, to get into a situation where such action would be necessary.

Having taken the necessary short-term action to support cashflow, Robin and his team set about putting together a plan for building the business over the coming years. However, owing to the financial situation facing the firm, it was necessary to gain support from the management committee before beginning the implementation. Although the London operation was a critical part of the global business, building it would require no small investment, and, in a business that faced the financial issues described earlier, it was by no means certain that support would be forthcoming to maintain the office. In early November, Robin, together with his two leadership colleagues, Crawford Gillies and Stan Miranda, took a presentation to the management committee, asking them to agree to keep the office open and to commit the funds which would stabilise the business. This meant, among other things, asking them effectively to agree to vote for lower compensation for themselves and all the other worldwide partners for the next few years. It was a measure of the seriousness of the situation that the committee was asked to take a vote; such behaviour was not typical of the management style of the firm.

Robin recalls the tenseness and the emotion of the meeting:

The outcome was by no means a foregone conclusion; the meeting was not short and the atmosphere was serious. I made the presentation of the plan on behalf of my leadership team and the decision as to how to proceed was put to the vote. The first four people voted to shut London down. In a financial situation as critical as ours was at the time, there is a strong argument for removing any part of the business which added to the difficulties. The fifth person to vote did so in our favour, commenting that, although he would not be prepared to bet on the plan, he was prepared to bet on the three of us! It was then the turn of Tom Tierney, who was then head of the California office whose partner group had seriously considered leaving the firm. He voted in favour of us. For him to have worked so hard to keep his own office in the firm and then to reach out to one of the weaker sisters was an extraordinarily brave move – one that I shall always thank him for.

Orit Gadeish lent her support also – 'I had known all along I could rely on her but it was still brilliant that she did!'

Eventually we won the vote 8 to 7. I shall never forget the moment! It taught me a key lesson about how people are prepared to support people and not plans or numbers. For me, it was also a clear demonstration of the extraordinary teaming that goes on within our firm and reconfirmed to me many of the reasons why I had decided to stay with the organisation.

Having won the support of the worldwide partners and the management committee, Robin and his team set about the task of rebuilding the business in London. Like the rest of the business, they focused primarily on their clients, setting out to deliver their extraordinary results for the businesses they worked with. The new team quickly realised that there were three key factors for success; client retention, sales wins and invitations to bid for projects. To build a truly sustainable business from where they were starting, they needed to acquire a reputation which meant that clients would come to them. All of this at a time when the UK was just entering a period which was to prove to be one of the deepest business recessions in years. This meant a fundamentally different approach to marketing and a commitment to rebuilding the team approach within the business.

Under Robin's guidance and with the strong support of Crawford Gillies and Stan Miranda, Paul Rogers and the other partners in the London office set out to re-establish its position within the business. Robin led the way in building a strategic marketing programme for the business, and step by step over the next ten years the business grew, not only in revenue terms but also in stature. In talking about the journey, Robin likened the period from 1990 to the present as not dissimilar to the experience of parenting an infant. Autumn 1990 represented a very difficult and painful birth process, while the next ten years mirrored a journey through childhood and adolescence until the office finally emerged as a fully fledged adult – a successful and sustainable business. On this journey, one of the important values that emerged was that of 'servant leadership'. Robin says:

> I take responsibility for importing the phrase 'servant leadership'. It absolutely describes our partner team at its best: epitomised by Crawford Gillies, managing partner of the London office; Tom Tierney and John Donahue, past and present worldwide managing directors; and Orit Gadeish in her leadership role with clients. It is someone who helps by leading others. It reminds me of the way my daughter 'leads' her younger brother. She reads to him, tells him stories, often with a moral, helps him with his homework, and acts as a role model. Not the bossy big sister, but the servant leader – someone who has earned the right to ask people to do things. As a business, we are extraordinarily lucky that we have a number of senior partners who have proved themselves able to provide such support to others when they have endured difficult times in their careers.
>
> Bain is a very special organisation; it is entrepreneurial and high energy, but most of all it is characterised by that gut thing that is about people and about teams!

Orit Gadeish – background and career path

Meanwhile, in the USA, with the financial reengineering underway, attention turned to the business transformation, and to re-establishing the revenues that had been achieved during the company's growth period. Here Orit Gadeish again enters the story.

Much has been written about Orit Gadeish. She has attracted significant press interest, not only for her style but also for her prominence in the world of management consultancy. She was elected chairman of Bain in 1993, because, according to Robin Buchanan, she was the individual most admired by her colleagues, and considered to be the best at what the consultancy delivered – that is, she was seen by the leadership team to be the client-facing role model, the consultant everyone in the business could aspire to be. Her reputation as a consultant was built on a combination of her outstanding business sense, her ability to see what the clients needed and to empathise with them in a direct, no nonsense way. As a result of her work with clients she recently ranked 26 in *Fortune*'s top 50 most powerful women.

The role of chairman at Bain is not an administrative position and Orit Gadeish is insistent in pointing out that the business is run in collegiate style. Although her role in the turnaround and transformation was a critical one, it was nonetheless part of a team effort, and she goes to great pains to ensure that undue credit is not laid at her door and that the role of other key players such as Tom Tierney and Robin Buchanan is understood and acknowledged.

Born in Haifa, Israel, she is the elder daughter of an Israeli general who helped professionalise the organisational structures of the Israeli army and later became the managing director of Monsanto's local subsidiary. She says she shares characteristics with both her parents, 'my father is a very successful business man, a general in the army, but very modest, very quiet. He has never been in the middle of anything. He never puts himself forward. My mother is completely the opposite. She is vivacious, funny, witty, and loves to be at the centre of attention.'

She grew up in Tel Aviv and initially hoped to be an urban planner, a career that sounded exciting in the still young state of Israel. At 17, to fulfil her compulsory military service, she joined the Israeli army. There are many rumours about her having been a tank commander, but in fact Gadeish spent two years in military intelligence as an aide to the deputy chief in charge of operations. This was a unique experience:

I worked very closely with all these generals in the war room. I learned at an early age to feel comfortable with some very respected people. It was a good place for me to grow up. I was there when some important things were happening around me, where life and death were very clear. You could see the impact of decisions and actions.

After completing her military service, Gadeish gave up her ideas of urban planning and instead enrolled at Hebrew University to study psychology. She completed her Bachelors degree and planned to take her doctorate and subsequently teach. But first she wanted to see the USA, and so secured for herself what she describes as a 'really uninteresting job' in the Israeli consulate in New York. While working here she met a Harvard Business School graduate, who convinced her she would be a good candidate for the MBA programme. Not yet fluent in English, she wrote her application in Hebrew, then translated it with help from her friends. Having secured a place, a year later she went on to graduate as a Baker Scholar, in the top five per cent of her class, as well as receiving the Brown Award for the most outstanding marketing student of her year. After graduating in 1977, she joined Bain as one of its first three women consultants.

She rapidly had impact at Bain, where she quickly developed an uncanny and unparalleled rapport with senior executives of some major American companies. As Robin puts it, 'she is the best active listener I have ever come across'.

In 1987, she was appointed executive vice-president, a position she held when the company hit its crisis. She was asked by Bill Bain to play a key role in managing the financial turnaround, a role she declined. She was instrumental in persuading Bill Bain to give the role of chairman to Mitt Romney. Of the role played by Mitt Romney, she comments:

> We emerged from that period with a strong balance sheet, a normal debt level comparable to a competitors and an ownership structure that is a true partnership. And we learnt tremendously important things in the process: about partnership, about governance of a professional services firm and about pride without arrogance.

In recalling her own feelings at the time, she says:

> It was awful. London was the most difficult place to be, followed by Boston. Boston was where the founders were and it was very visible what was happening on a day-to-day basis.

> As a management committee, we decided to focus on the three most important assets of any consulting firm, namely clients, people and reputation – all were in jeopardy.

> The client side proved to be the most straightforward – the product delivered by Bain continued to add value and, despite a 'tricky period' and the best efforts of competitors, the firm continued to win beauty contests and build new businesses while maintaining its existing client base. During this period, no single client was lost. The firm's reputation had been damaged by the Guinness affair, but the decision was made to continue to pursue excellence and deliver greater results for the client. By focusing externally rather than internally, there was a strong belief that reputation would be rebuilt, particularly if supported by a strong marketing programme.

On the people side, things were more difficult. 'Everyone was talking to head hunters and openly talking about the fact that they were doing so! Our collective pride had gone.'

Like everyone else, she, too, was taking calls from headhunters but, after talking to a colleague who commented 'not that I want to leave Bain – I just don't want be the last one left,' she made a commitment to stay with the business for the next two years. It was a very decisive moment. 'I called back every headhunter who had called me and told them not to ring me again. I would not be leaving.' This was not a decision without risk, as it was by no means certain what the future would be, but Orit says: 'The next time someone said to me "everyone is talking to headhunters" this allowed me to truthfully say I'm not talking to anyone – I'm staying.'

Winning hearts and minds

It was an important moment in the transformation, as was the moment when another partner told her that he had decided to stay. Orit asked him to talk publicly about his decision – to tell people that he had considered leaving but had decided to stay and why. These were important watershed moments, but in the spring of 1992, a year and a half into the turnaround, Orit realised that there was still something missing. She recognised the need to focus on reinstalling a collective sense of pride and confidence in the company. 'By pride I meant a conviction that what Bain had set out to do was really worth doing, a conviction that enough of us were still passionate about what we did. This shared passion was what had once made this place great. I was sure we could do it again.' So after consulting with colleagues, Orit made a speech to the USA practice in August 1992 which has gone down in history of the company. Historically, presentations to the business had always been highly rational, relying on charts and graphs. Analytical speeches worked well. Gadeish believed that effecting a pride turnaround required a different type of speech and consequently she broke the mould and talked about what working for the company meant to her. She did not use numbers or charts, nor did she use many overheads but rather talked about her pride in what she did and in the people she worked with. Using examples to illustrate their achievements, Gadeish urged her colleagues to once again feel good about what they were doing. Crawford Gillies, who was present at a time, said 'She did an incredible job articulating what it meant to be part of Bain. It was a visible manifestation of what leadership is all about.'

Orit said: 'I wanted it be personal on my part, and personal to everyone else in the room – intuitively I knew it was the right thing to do.' The speech – which came to be known as the 'Pride Turnaround' speech – is credited as a turning point in effecting a new confidence throughout the company and, as a result many consider Orit to be the spiritual backbone of the organisation. Later she captured the importance of values, to herself and to Bain, in what has become known as her 'True North' speech. In describing the importance of values she said:

> We have all used a compass to navigate. Most of us use an ordinary compass. But an ordinary compass points to magnetic north, and the direction of magnetic north changes, it depends on both the time and your location. If you really need to know where you are, you need a gyro compass that works on its own internal system rather than the external system of the very fickle magnetic field. Magnetic north is fine for an afternoon walk, but if you're on a stormy ocean, the winds are shifting and you're running out of food and water, you'd better know where true north is or you may not survive!

> True north is what ultimately defines an organisation and its core values. It's what guides people as they make decisions on the margins. It's what should eventually be predictable about an organisation, even if it is hard to stick to at times. It's actions, not words... and its dissemination within the organisation is what ultimately forms the basis for trust.

> In fact you only really know you have true north when trade-offs have had to be made, when your organisation has been tested, and it has emerged from the test still holding on to the same values.

Orit Gadeish talks of the pride she has in the company and the individuals within it. When asked what is it that makes Bain special for her, she replied:

> My colleagues are pure pleasure; they're smart, they're fun – it is a real privilege to work with them.

The focus of Orit, Robin and their colleagues on these values and the team approach has resulted in one of the great success stories of consulting. The shared values meant that each of the partners knew that their colleagues would be there when they needed them and that each of them would make the same judgement call, even the toughest ones, when the chips were down. Since 1990, Bain has successfully transformed itself from being a consultancy run by its founders to being a professional global partnership – and it has grown to four times its previous size. Its reputation with its clients for analytical rigour and results is enviable and it continues to be the company of choice for many top graduates from the elite business schools. In a 1998 survey in the USA Bain was placed at the top of the list for client satisfaction.

Part III

Part III

11 Themes from the Cases

Our starting point

Before putting this section into context, it is worth going back to the beginning. The idea for this book came from the observation of the gap between the leader most often portrayed in the popular media – the super-hero who could leap tall buildings in a single bound – and the individual we had encountered time and again in consulting to businesses undergoing significant change.

Our experience was that these people were not a race apart, impervious to and untouched by the kaleidoscope of emotions that impinge on, and often handicap, all of us during our working lives, but rather that the opposite was in many ways true. These were individuals who were special because they had somehow managed to cope with the difficulties and to harness these 'human reactions', focusing them in a way which allowed them to deliver extraordinary things, both through the application of their own skills and the engagement of the human resources around them.

Furthermore, we should reiterate that this is not a study with any kind of statistical significance, but rather a compilation of stories told by a group of individuals who have been instrumental in seeing through extraordinary changes in their organisations – who have seen their dreams become a reality.

Therefore this section is not an attempt to pigeonhole any or all of our interviewees and impose upon them common characteristics or attributes where these do not exist. Rather, it is to reflect upon our sample and what they have said; in order to see if there is anything they share in terms of background, personality and experience that has impacted on and influenced their leadership style and their ability to drive change.

The intention is not to distil a recipe for success, but rather to reflect the mirror back onto the narrative given by these leaders to see what, if any, common themes lie within their stories. This is in the spirit of understanding a story as it seems to make sense to us and, hopefully, as a result, to provide a perspective which may prove useful when confronting the conundrum that faces each of us: 'you can only understand life backwards, but you have to live it forwards.'

Diversity

The first, and most striking, thing that must be noted about this, admittedly small, sample is the diversity – our interviewees share little in terms of background, culture, birth position, industry or class. However, they are all united by their lifelong commitment to making a difference and by their achievements in having successfully delivered transformational and sustainable change in their chosen industry.

The things that shaped them

Most of them enjoyed a strong relationship with their parents; a relationship which was supportive, encouraging and focused on the child as an individual (in transactional analysis terms, this relationship would best be described as 'adult'). Our sample often talked of these relationships as being mutually loving, and as something which continued to be a sustaining factor throughout their career. These supportive backgrounds seem to have contributed to early emotional maturity. This strength has been a prime factor in driving many of their achievements.

Our sample enjoyed varying educational experiences and academic achievements. None chose to pursue well-trodden or 'labelled' (professional) careers, and few of them articulated any early career plans. Rather, most of them spent their early years in pursuit of something they felt passionately about. This passion was later intuitively channelled into an area where they believed they could make a difference; where they could leave something better than it had been when they found it. In a number of cases, the industry which they chose as their canvas was intuitive, almost an accidental choice.

It would be difficult to describe any of our sample as being ambitious in the traditional sense. They were driven much more by doing the right thing than by any focus on achieving status or personal reward. Personal ego was much less important and therefore much less fragile than a belief in making things better and a commitment to making a difference – implicitly, from their early career they preferred to be judged against their legacy rather than their current position.

Making a difference – a vision

From early on, most of the stories tell of a belief in, and a commitment to, making a difference. Once in the world of work, this commitment quickly translated into a vision as to how things might be better, what the future could be like. This vision, almost without exception, broke the existing mould. It was not concerned with improving the present via tinkering, but rather it envisaged a much more radical future, quite removed from the status quo. In thinking through this vision, they were not impeded by sacred cows or other existing barriers – they simply blue-skied 'the art of the possible'. In doing this, they felt their way towards what it would take to succeed; what it was that their customers really wanted. Their vision was often not 'buttoned-down', but more likely to be only directionally correct – a 'broad canvas'.

This, then, provided a beacon for their career, a touchstone for the future. Few of them felt they had to have the final answer at the outset; they were happy to see the details emerge over time, and for others to 'fill in the trees and rivers'. They trusted they would know the right answer when they saw it, and consequently were able to live with considerable ambiguity.

Relating to others

Each instinctively demonstrated a strong belief in other people, particularly those lower down the organisation, 'those closest to the customer'. They have a natural tendency to empower and trust. Many have strong communication skills and consequently they were good at gaining support. As a result, they often had strong and personal relationships with those who worked for them and were often able to inspire unusual loyalty.

On achieving leadership positions, a number, either organisationally or more informally, removed previous hierarchies to reduce the distance between themselves and the grassroots of the organisation in order to ensure they stayed in touch with what was happening at the sharp end. Indeed, most had worked their way up through the hierarchy.

Somewhat in contrast, their relationship with their peers was always highly professional and often aloof or distant. Typically, each of them maintained a strict separation between work and outside life with few, if any, social relationships crossing the boundaries. Although, without exception, both socially skilled and sociable, our sample are intensely private individuals, fiercely protective of their privacy.

Emphasis on values

Our sample share a number of personal attributes. Each of them has demonstrated a high level of integrity, honesty, intelligence, energy and an almost childlike curiosity. They have a strong and enduring sense of responsibility, and are highly conscientious and focused in pursuit of a goal. They value excellence in their own work and expect it from others. This focus on excellence was a key factor in allowing them to reach beyond the immediate – in striving for results they were prepared to take risks and do new things. This included a willingness to change themselves when necessary.

Most have demonstrated a strong self-reliance and each values their own intuition. While all of them are naturally analytical, particularly in the process of discovery, they typically use data to support an intuition or a hypothesis – rarely starting with a blank sheet. Their visions, while eventually analytically robust, were first based on an intuitive feel for what might be achieved.

Furthermore, this intuition is very evident in all of their dealings with people. Here, they often demonstrate intuition and insight and an engaging ability to empathise with others. Typically, they tend to trust in others, believing the best of an individual, and are prepared to delegate and empower. They are not over-concerned with personal power, and openly acknowledge what they do not know – they tend to view this not as a weakness, but as an opportunity for learning. None of them feel the need to have all the answers to bolster their self-confidence. Rather each demonstrates a refreshing openness to learning. When under pressure, they have absolute belief in themselves and are strongly self-reliant. Yet, when circumstances point to the need to do something differently, a number of them have demonstrated a willingness and ability to change their behaviours and approach.

It is striking in talking to the leaders that there is a strong congruence between their personal values and their business values. As a result, they do not have to adopt an uncomfortable persona, or play a role, at work, but rather the different parts of their lives fit together without conflict.

They typically value simplicity. Their naturally intuitive approach is further reflected in their tendency to think and talk in pictures. This gives them the ability to put across highly complex concepts and ideas in a way that can be more easily understood by others – they have little time for buzzwords or management fads. This ability to simplify has proved an important tool in their leadership kitbag. It can inspire curiosity and generate enthusiasm in others and has been an important factor in mobilising organisations behind them and their vision.

Handling pressure

We have already noted the congruence between their personal and their business values – this appears to be a major factor in their ability to overcome the difficulties and emotions of delivering change; in other words in their ability to 'take the strain'. It has removed the need for role-playing, with a subsequent reduction in the stress that many people can experience if they have, in effect, to be different people in different parts of their life.

It is also striking that a number of them enjoy a significant and absorbing interest outside work, which has often been an important safety valve for them. While the issues and challenges at work may have been totally absorbing and dominating on an intellectual basis, this outside interest has often provided relief on an emotional level. This has given them the opportunity to 'switch off' emotionally. As a result, they have found the stresses and strains of their workload less threatening to them as individuals. This has contributed to their ability to achieve extraordinary things.

Most of them have enjoyed a strong and stable home life, building on the foundations of their childhood background. As a consequence, in pursuing their vision they have not typically been compensating for something lacking in their personal lives, but rather the different parts of their lives have combined to allow them to 'realise a dream'. Their work commitments have often not allowed them to play more than a peripheral role in family life, and they recognise that they and their families have had to pay a price for this. For those who have now entered the retirement phase of their careers, the family has now taken a much more central role. This is allowing them to give back to the families who have given so much, and particularly to their partners. These partners have often acted as informal mentors throughout their careers, fulfilling the role of confidante and sounding board as appropriate, often providing a perspective that has been important in handling the pressure.

Leaving a legacy

As is clear from their stories, our individuals were strongly driven by the wish to leave a legacy – this legacy being inspired more by revolution than by evolution. In contrast to many an entrepreneur, these leaders were committed at an early stage to seeing this legacy extend beyond their own tenure. This long-term focus is an important factor in explaining their approach to a number of issues.

Their focus on sustainability breeds a willingness to let go and move aside when appropriate, since they are not wedded to status or position. They each have highly developed skills and intuitions for spotting talent. In trusting individuals, they often exhibit an unusual innocence, taking things at face value. They see things as about roles and not about positions and do not waste time politicking. They instinctively and by experience value team-work but are more typically used to playing the role of captain. Their instinct is to take charge, but to use the team around them to deliver against a goal.

Observations

In characterising our individuals, a number of conclusions can be drawn:

- Each of them has a strong rational bias, particularly when under stress, yet none seek to exclude the emotional reaction either in themselves or in others.

- Each behaves in a very 'human' way, without often demonstrating strong emotional swings. Rather, each shows a strong and enduring emotional stability.

- Each demonstrates a strong congruence in behaviour, values and emotions inside and outside of work.

- Each passionately believes in the General Patton model of leadership – 'if you tell people where to go, but not how to get there, you will be amazed at the results'.

There are a number of similarities with the Peters and Waterman concept of excellence; a bias for action (not analysis), a belief in the need to stick close to the customer, a belief in delivery and progress through people, simplicity, focus, an intuitive leaning towards leanness and nimbleness, and the belief in helping everyone to know their place and role.

Our observations confirm many of the learnings of the formal studies of leaders undertaken over time. Many of the characteristics observed here have previously been identified, but what we believe to be new here is the strong focus on 'being human'. The 'specialness' we alluded to at the beginning boils down, in our view, to being 'human' – by this we mean being subject to, and in tune with, the emotional roller-coaster that accompanies change, and the ability to deal with it in a way which is empathetic to those involved, and which does not compromise the leader.

Our conclusion – the so what?

Our simple conclusion is that leaders who successfully deliver change are similar to the rest of us in many respects, and yet quite different from us in many others. They can leverage their own emotions to effect making a difference and, in overcoming barriers, they can connect with, and leverage, the emotions of others. These leaders do not have different expectations, hopes, fears or concerns from the rest of us. But they do have a different focus, particularly in the arena of change. They simply do not 'see' many of the barriers around change that others do. Rather it is their focus on the future that allows them to do extraordinary things, overcoming what to most others would be impossible barriers.

12 The Challenges Faced by Leaders are Changing

The qualities of 21st-century leadership

The 21st-century leader has to be able to meet a number of changing expectations from within and from outside the organisation.

Even more than today, a leader will need to be capable of creating and communicating a vision, of providing a binding and compelling sense of purpose, of holding together loose and shifting networks and alliances, and of making change happen.

Warren Bennis[1] talks of leaders having to 'keep recomposing and reinventing their leadership' which presupposes that they 'have enough self-awareness and self-esteem to sense when a different repertoire of competencies will be needed, without being threatened by the need to change'.

It goes without saying that leaders will have to be able to cope with the stresses of the role. In addition to loneliness, there are other pressures identified by Sadler:[2] such as status anxiety (wanting to be simultaneously respected and popular); the difficulty of maintaining a personal identity; and the problem of achieving a balance between work and home.

Emotional competence will remain an important topic for businesses. For the leaders themselves, it will have a double importance. First, in terms of their personal well-being and capabilities, for it is unlikely that a leader will be effective at influencing the well-being of the whole organisation, in an emotional or in any other sense, unless they are capable of understanding and meeting their own needs first. Second, in terms of their ability to create a climate, through their example, personal values and inspiration, which can affect the organisation as a whole, and is critical if the organisation is to change.

These personal needs are to do both with finding the inner resources to lead change and avoiding the pitfalls of leadership.

How the leaders we talked to have shown the way ahead

Finding a purpose

In writing about the importance of having a purpose, and of it being outside ourselves, in the sense of not being self-seeking, Charles Handy likens our existence to that of 'a sparrow flying through a dark hall',[3] which powerfully evokes a feeling of disorientation. The sense of direction, or vision as it is often called in business, often starts from what ignites a passion within us personally.

For example, Tim Waterstone's vision of a different and better sort of bookshop and drive to outdo WHSmith clearly provided a powerful focus and purpose for his organisation.

Orit Gadeish's 'Pride Turnaround' speech was both a very personal statement about her values and a rallying point for Bain and Company at a critical time in its struggle for survival.

Spotlighting problems

One of the hardest tasks for a change leader is to move an organisation out of denial, which is often why a profit crisis is needed before there is acceptance that change is needed, by which time it may be too late.

One of the biggest challenges that Cor Herkstroter and then Mark Moody Stewart have faced in the second half of the 1990s at Royal Dutch Shell, an organisation of great strengths but generally agreed to be in need of updating its management processes, has been the inertia generated by sustained profitability.

It is no coincidence that one of Jack Welch's themes is 'change before you have to', and that he believes that change must 'start with reality. Get all the facts out'[4] – both of which can only be initiated by the leader, and may require considerable courage and persistance.

For example, Ian MacLaurin led the critical relaunch of Tesco at the time of the dropping of Green Shield stamps in the teeth of strong opposition from the founding fathers, who had lost contact with what was actually going on in the stores. It had taken an unprecedented challenge in the boardroom to bring home the reality.

When he took over the VW business in the UK, Richard Ide found himself at the head of an organisation with a massive degree of self-satisfaction, but which was in fact surrounded by a host of internal and external issues. A strong wake-up call was needed.

For Ashok Ganguly, his frustration with the arrogance and remoteness of scientists from commercial realities led to a lifelong crusade to strengthen the connection between science and business.

Despite the emotional drain, the short-term actions that Robin Buchanan and his partners took to reduce costs in the London office were unavoidable if the business was to survive.

Empathy – being connected

Change leaders depend on being able to engage the hearts as well as the minds of the organisation. This is greatly helped by an ability to empathise with what people at all levels are feeling – 'effective leaders put words to the formless feelings and deeply felt needs of others'.[5]

For example, the way in which the Bain and Company partner team led the rebuilding of the London office through 'servant leadership' exemplifies the sensitive nature of the leadership role in a high-performing organisation – one which is based on close understanding of the needs of the individuals being led, rather than on those of the leader.

Tapping into the suppressed emotional energy

If a leader needs to engage the emotions of others, they need first to engage their own. It may be possible to arouse strong feelings in others about a change programme, say, without feeling strongly about it yourself, but it is unlikely.

For example, the kind of culture Tim Waterstone created in his organisation, at least during the time of its fastest growth in the early years, was one which powerfully engaged the individual – no hierarchy, direct communication, family-orientated and personal.

Ashok Ganguly made a priority at Hindustan Lever of creating the right conditions in which people, both as individuals and teams, could give of their best.

Providing security during transition

The biggest barrier to the acceptance of the need for change, and of the need to do something about it, is the instinctive fear that the prospect of change arouses in us. The evolutionary psychologists trace this to our need for security – we are conditioned to react to any change as a potential threat and our instinct is to opt for the status quo, which is safer.

During change, the leader him- or herself plays a vital part in meeting our basic need for security. Dave Ulrich says that the leader's role is to 'create the emotional bond needed in times of rapid and turbulent change'.[6]

For themselves

Being able to change him- or herself

Being able to evolve in line with new conditions and new roles is critical in times of change. On this theme, John O'Neil writes: 'Real change on the organisational level has to begin with real change inside leaders.'[7] This is echoed by Warren Bennis, who says: 'What distinguishes a leader from everyone else is that he takes all of that [nature and nurture] and makes himself – all new and unique.'[8]

Surviving turbulence

A key success factor for the leaders of change is the self-confidence and resilience which enables them to stay on an even keel, whatever the circumstances. Failing this, they need the courage to know that they are going to survive the white water. They may need to make changes of plan, or even temporary changes in direction, but these will be accomplished with the knowledge that this will not be life-threatening.

Protecting themselves against stress

A leader, as do many others in business, has to protect him- or herself against the point at which their own drive to succeed, the pressure from competition, or from the expectations of others, create stress rather than stimulus. He or she has to protect him- or herself against the point at which the balance, whether it is between energy and workload, fun and duty, or work and personal life, is lost.

For example, each of those we have talked to has been able to put a clear dividing line between themselves and the business when they needed to. Tim Waterstone made a point of going home at a reasonable hour to

bath his young children and read them a bedtime story. He also spent an
hour and a half each day on his own writing.

Avoiding 'derailment'

Apart from stress, there are other psychological risks, which Manfred Kets
de Vries[9] identifies, facing a leader by virtue of their position, such as
being isolated, or being idealised by the organisation. To avoid these, as
well as to retain a sense of personal identity, the leader has to deliberately
seek mechanisms for keeping in touch with reality.

For the organisation

Role modelling personal change for others

For change to percolate through an organisation, individual change on the
part of many people at all levels must take place. But before they make
that change, many will look to the leader as a role model.

For example, Richard Ide led the transformation of VW from the front
and by personal example. With the help of a coach, he, along with the rest
of the board, confronted his personal strengths and weaknesses, and
adapted his style to become less of a hands-on manager and more of a
leader, perceived as less distant and more approachable.

Ashok Ganguly set an example of being prepared to make significant
personal change and accept the risks involved when he decided to return
to India from Europe and transfer from research to manufacturing, even
though it felt like restarting his career after eight years with the company
and moving a couple of steps down the pecking order.

Forming a fulfilling and creative work culture

Independent of the need to adapt to change, there will be increasing
expectations of personal fulfilment from our workplace. One viewpoint,
represented by John O'Neil, following E.F. Schumacher in *Small Is Beau-*
tiful (Vintage, 1993), is that this will come from a greater balance
between work and relaxation. This is not in the sense of spending more
time than we do at the moment on the one, and less on the other, but on
being able to experience each differently: 'It means approaching work

with the same joyously energetic spirit we bring to play, and applying the same dedication and seriousness of purpose valued in the workplace to our personal lives.'[10]

For O'Neil, the challenge for a leader is to modify their organisation in a way which encourages this, and to set an example by leading a more balanced life themselves.

Being an effective coach and developer

Whatever else a future leader may need to do, it is probable that, with a devolution of responsibility and less hierarchical management, his or her ability to achieve results through coaching, that is, through helping others to bring out the best in themselves, will become more important.

An effective coach, according to coaching expert Eric Parsloe,[11] needs several 'personal' skills, in addition to 'core' skills (such as listening and observation) and 'technique' skills (such as the ability to adapt coaching style to the preferred learning style). These 'personal' skills include the ability to:

■ display sensitivity to and empathy for the learner's thoughts and ideas and understand the need for appropriate feedback
■ establish rapport and good communication channels with the learner
■ encourage the learner to take responsibility for his or her own development
■ support and build confidence in the learner

and are based on what others might well call emotional capability.

13 The Context for Leadership has Changed

Although many of the leadership requirements are similar to those faced when transforming businesses during the latter part of the last millennium, the context within which the change needs to happen will be significantly different.

Leaders will increasingly have to deal with pressures on the individual, and on the organisation, which derive from the changing nature of society, and from the way in which our businesses are continuing to evolve.

Pressures on the individual

The increasing power of the individual

Both in business, and as a consumer, the individual is becoming increasingly the centre of focus. This is partly because of organisational changes which promote empowerment, and partly because of the power which information technology brings. As a consumer, the individual is being empowered by the Internet. By enabling us to communicate our wants directly to the manufacturer, whether it's the ability to specify directly the components we need in our Dell computer or to compare manufacturers' prices at the touch of a button, the Internet is already redefining the nature of customer relationships, and making mass customisation a reality in a number of industries.

Within an information age business, the contribution, hence the value, of an individual is greater than it ever has been.

Living with discontinuity

The consensus of those who think and write about the future seems to be that one thing we can be sure of is discontinuity. Not only is change taking place faster than ever before, but the future will not be like the past.

For example, Charles Handy says: 'You can't look at the future as a continuation of the past... because the future is going to be different.'[1] Although, he says, with many of the institutions, such as work organisations, which shape our lives disappearing, the one thing the future will contain is uncertainty: 'Life seems to be a succession of open-ended problems with no right answers.'[2] Handy sees the collapse of traditional authority as taking us to the edge of chaos, which may stimulate and enable creativity, 'but it's also by definition a very troubled, very difficult time and place'.[3]

New organisations

As we speed from the industrial age through the information age, not only are companies like ABB and Virgin seeking to operate through smaller, family-sized business units, but some leaders, like Ricardo Semler, are tearing up the rule books completely. At Semco, he and his employees have created what he describes in his book *Maverick!*, 'a more humane, trusting, productive, exhilarating, and in every sense, rewarding way'[4] of running a business. Through an extreme example of participative management, the wishes and abilities of individual workers take precedence in the way the businesses are run, and the bottom-line results are staggering – growth up sixfold, productivity up nearly sevenfold, and profits up fivefold.[5]

The Times summarised some effects of these new organisations on the individual thus:

> Hierarchies are being replaced by networks; labour and management are uniting; wages are coming in new mixtures of options, incentives and ownership; fixed job skills are giving way to lifelong learning as fixed jobs melt into fluid careers.[6]

The conclusion is that, to be successful in this new, delayered, empowered world, new skills are needed, and consequently that individuals who work in these environments want to be led by a different sort of leader, one who will have the human capability of being in touch with them as individuals. However, as we have seen, these traits are far from new. Evolutionary psychology, a recently emerging science which combines genetics, neuropsychology, and paleobiology, contends that natural selection has hardwired a number of traits into all of us, including the way we think and feel.

Evolutionary psychologists would endorse the pursuit by industrialists such as Percy Barnevik (at ABB) and Sir Richard Branson (at Virgin) of human-scale business units. According to Robin Dunbar of the University of Liverpool[7], the biggest number of people that a human-size brain can handle (that is, manage all the complex relationships required for survival) is 150.

Handling the pressures of devolved and flexible organisations

As companies pursue streamlined operations and faster decision-making based closer to the customer, organisations are being created which feel very different to work in from the old hierarchies. These new organisations are not just smaller business units, but delayered structures in which people are expected to carry accountability and take decisions that their bosses would traditionally have taken. People may be grouped according to how the work needs to be done, rather than by functional allegiance; they may work in project-based teams which come together for a particular purpose and then disband; or in virtual organisations based around the world, and held together by voice and e-mail, and by intranets.

What do these new organisations feel like to work in? Warren Bennis[8] believes that increasing rates of change will make organisations 'confusing, chaotic places to work in'.

Although for some the lack of definition may feel truly empowering, for others it may feel like more pressure, more risk and more uncertainty – and this is independent of where you reside in the hierarchy.

It is not as though empowerment is a one-off decision, which enables managers to concentrate on something else with a certain peace of mind. The reality can be continuous discomfort. Peter Senge[9] describes how top managers will push down decisions for a while, but, when the going gets tough, insecurity makes them pull them back in again.

It does not necessarily seem to be getting any easier. Many commentators see the future organisation as more of a network than a hierarchy, with the principal clarifying and binding mechanism being the common culture, underpinned by vastly improved information technology.

Senge[10] cites Visa International as an example, which is a network organisation rather like a club, with a set of operating principles but no hierarchy. It is the kind of organisation described by Visa International's founder, Dee Hock, as 'chaordic', that is, one which generates order out of chaos, rather than seeking to impose order on chaos.

In fact, this new terminology is typical of the assumption among observers that organisations are moving so far from the traditional that we are running out of ways to describe them. For example, Charles Handy had to invent the concept of the 'inverted doughnut' in order to explain how companies differentiate between core and non-core activities. Others have had to resort to political or biological analogies, or to chaos theory.

The need to develop new behaviours

New forms of organisations will create their own new rules and new critical success factors. For example, the less well defined the organisation structure, and the more frequently it changes, the more critical will be the ability to network in order to build relationships with those in power.

The need to use all our senses

In an increasingly competitive world, we will need to utilise all our capabilities to the full. Kets de Vries says that executives will need to be able to balance rational, analytical approaches with intuitive thinking processes in order to extract the most information from a situation:

> They will have to cultivate the ability to interpret the kind of feelings that can be stirred up in interpersonal situations. The emotional agenda in professional encounters is often glossed over. Excellent executives, however, pay attention to these processes, which they see as extra pieces of information.[11]

Managing our own careers

While the power of the individual has increased, so too has the responsibility. Just as the empowered employee now has to take responsibility for business decisions rather than passing them upwards, he or she also has to take responsibility for his or her own career and development.

At a time of unprecedented turbulence – when companies rise and fall faster than ever before, when the 'career for life' has disappeared, and when commentators say that downsizing has reduced the number of friendly mentors available to provide good counsel – the individual has to rely on his or her own resources to plot a course through what is likely to be a multi-stage journey.

This will certainly require a high level of self-reliance, but it will also need to be informed by continuing self-awareness.

Pressures on business leaders

Avoiding derailment

Business leaders are at risk psychologically through the very nature of their position. The same strong self-belief (Warren Bennis's 'positive self-regard') and determination which are essential to get to the top of an organisation may, once the leader has got there, lead to conditions of hubris or of narcissism, in which the leader behaves, or is expected to behave, as though they are perfect and infallible.

Kets de Vries[12] identifies three forces which may cause leaders to derail: being isolated, they are unable to have their own needs for contact, support and reassurance met and may lose contact with reality; employees' conscious and unconscious expectations of the leader may be too much of a burden; or leaders may unconsciously cause themselves to fail through guilt feelings about their success.

The paradox for the business leader is that while he or she is potentially under greater psychological risk, they are at the same time less able to get help when they need it – having been trained to present 'an image of invulnerability and vitality',[13] it becomes harder to admit to such 'weaknesses' as stress and depression when things do not go right. Being isolated at the top of the organisation, there are fewer people to reach out to.

Avoiding the delusions of success

For John O'Neil, unrealistic aspirations also present a high risk. What he calls 'mythic success' contains a number of delusions – that success is absolute and final; that money is central to success; that we must succeed more than others, or that they must fail; that envy can be avoided; that success makes you free.[14]

Pressures on employers

Meeting new, non-material expectations from employment

As the leverage of the individual becomes more significant, the individual's wants and needs become more critical for businesses to understand and action. As we have seen earlier, there are signs that these are evolving away from the purely material in the way that Maslow predicted.

One thing that some people are looking for from their work is a greater sense of fulfilment. Stephen Covey[15] puts it thus:

> You have to help people find meaning and fulfilment in what they do. They don't want to be 'used' by the organisation like victims or pawns. They want to have stewardship over their own resources. They want to feel that they are making a personal contribution to something meaningful. And that's when you get real motivation and real fulfilment.

For Charles Handy,[16] this means 'If you want to retain talent you've got to create a cause'.

It is as though we are in some way climbing an organisational hierarchy of needs that maps the individual's hierarchy. In other words, the initial concern of an organisation is survival, but, once the basics of survival have been attended to by management, then the higher-order, more intangible elements – such as self-fulfilment, values, ethics, even spirituality – need to be addressed by leadership.

The need to stimulate creativity

The faster the pace of change, the greater the need for creativity at work. However, pay is not enough to stimulate creativity by itself. A survey by Aon Consulting, quoted in *Fortune*,[17] says that pay ranks 11th as a creator of workforce commitment. What is really critical, say the evolutionary psychologists, to unleashing the creative instinct is not incentives, but conditions which meet our emotional needs for security. In other words, we are creative when we enjoy what we are doing. But if we are not secure, we will not be imaginative. Michael Eisner, CEO of the Walt Disney Company, says: 'Being in connection with our emotional depths is critical to releasing our most powerful and creative forces.'[18]

Pressures on society

The stress epidemic

Businesses also have to contend with background factors which are affecting the society from which their employees are drawn, one of which is a rise in stress. Oliver James, in *Britain On The Couch*, maps out a significant increase in depression since the Second World War across the developed world to a level that he considers equivalent to an epidemic.

What is behind this? For Oliver James, one main cause is our failure to live up to the aspirations set for us by our upbringing and the way we compare ourselves to others:

> Since 1950, expectations have risen dramatically for personal and professional fulfilment... Likewise, demands for individualism have inflated. The media... increased hours spent at school and competitiveness there and increased pressure to compete at work make us obsessively preoccupied with how we are doing compared to others and whether we are individual enough.[19]

Part IV

Part IV

14 Practical Steps Towards Developing Our Human Side

This section in perspective

We believe two things need to be said to put this section into perspective. First, there is no easy or simple route to increasing our ability to operate as fully authentic human beings. Second, even if there were, it would not in and of itself enable someone to be as effective a leader as those we have talked to, since clearly they possess a number of other critical qualities.

However, since there may be some who wonder what steps they might take to start building their, and their organisation's, emotional capability, we are including an overview of some of the steps that this might involve. (An overview is, of course, just that. For more detail read the authors cited.)

Emotional capability

It is worth first clarifying what is meant by 'emotional competence or capability'. Most writers and practitioners divide it into two – how we manage our own emotional capability, and how we use our own capability to increase the effectiveness of our interaction with others.

Managing our own capability depends fundamentally on a heightened awareness of our own feelings, and enables us to control or limit the impact of our negative emotions, such as fear and anger, and to channel our feelings in a positive direction, such as increasing our motivation.

The basic building block for increased effectiveness in working with those around us is our ability to empathise with them (which in turn is based on our increased self-awareness). The more we understand how others are feeling, the better we will be at communicating with them, influencing them, co-operating with them, or supporting them.

Potential areas of benefit

There are three broad ways in which encouraging greater emotional competency may reward a leader who makes it a priority, three levels, so to speak, in the hierarchy of emotional leverage. On the most basic level, greater emotional literacy in an organisation is likely to promote greater emotional well-being, that is, the avoidance of the emotional negatives, such as stress and derailment.

Then there is the level of change. Whether it is self-development or renewal at the individual level, or the transformation of an organisation, the issue is how to recognise the importance of the emotional dimension during change, for example in overcoming resistance, tapping into deeply held values and harnessing latent energy.

At the highest level, there is the potential for maximising the upside of putting in place a culture of cooperation and interpersonal capability, which will meet both the company's need for creative collaboration and the individual's need for fulfilment in their work.

Two dimensions

For a business leader, therefore, the question has two dimensions – the personal and the organisational. The first relates to their own growth, renewal and development and the second to what they can do for their organisation as a whole. The two dimensions are interrelated; for example, to be able to change the organisation the leader has to start with him- or herself. Thus a manager said of Jack Welch in Tichy and Sherman's account[1] of the transformation of GE:

> The company had a tremendous need to change, so you needed a different kind of person – a change agent – to come in. But if that change agent had not been able to change himself, how could you trust him to change the company.

The personal dimension: self-change

The good news is that we can change ourselves. In *Working With Emotional Intelligence*, Daniel Goleman[2] says that 'all emotional competencies can be cultivated with the right practice'. The rather more challenging news is that because such learning is experiential, not only does it take time, but also a number of conditions have to be right for it to succeed – Goleman lists no less than 15 criteria for effective emotional competency training.

Much has been written about self-change – there are many approaches, and many, what appear to be, impossibly instant recipes. In essence, to change ourselves we have to learn – not just about where we are now, but about how to do things differently. Expressed in more personal terms, we have to learn about *who* we are now, and how to *be*, or *behave*, differently.

Routes to learning

Learning about ourselves can, like any other form of learning, be carried out formally through executive training, or less formally through personalised coaching and development programmes. It can even be achieved, for some, through self-managed learning, using books such as those listed in the Bibliography as a guide.

Formal learning

As an example of a training programme which meets his success criteria, Daniel Goleman cites, in *Working with Emotional Intelligence,*[3] the Managerial Assessment and Development course which Richard Boyatzis leads for MBA students at Weatherhead School of Management at Case Western Reserve University in Cleveland, Ohio.

The students, who can either be on an MBA course, or older professionals taking a special one-year course, start by reflecting on their values and aspirations. Much emphasis is placed on taking stock, goal-setting and planning. The first two of the weekly three-hour sessions are focused on assessing strengths and weaknesses, and then a further seven sessions on digesting the results, after which five weeks are spent developing learning plans.

Informal learning

An analogy often used about change is that of a journey, which implies elements of unpredictability, endurance and elapsed time. We have to provide our own motivation to embark on it, we have to choose our direction, set our goals and take responsibility for keeping ourselves moving forward. The whole process is made easier if there is someone to travel with us, whether they act as a guide or simply as a companion with whom to share experiences.

Who we choose to take on the journey is important. Family and friends certainly have our best interests at heart, and have a valuable role to play, such as providing frank feedback and supporting us at critical moments, but there are also factors which limit their ability to contribute. We have relationships with them which are already complex enough without the extra burden of becoming our change support as well, nor do they have the experience of having travelled the road before, or the objectivity. On a journey such as this, it will help to have a specialist guide such as a coach, counsellor, mentor or therapist.

The learning cycle

Whichever route you take, the components are broadly the same:

1. Take stock and begin to build self-awareness
2. Identify change needs and set goals
3. Practice
4. Ask for feedback
5. Make sure you have support throughout.

The difficult bit – getting started

For many of us, embarking on such a process can be difficult. We may not feel an urgent need to embark voluntarily on a journey of this sort – often it is only when it is forced on us by some major life event, or career crisis, that we accept the inevitable. It could be that we don't see ourselves as being worth bothering about in this way. We can be so busy playing multiple roles (career person, spouse, parent, friend) that sometimes we can overlook our own needs, or we may consider that we are of lesser priority.

Sometimes we do feel the need, but stifle the prompting. We would rather not look too closely in the mirror, for fear of what we may see. Nor will we welcome the risk of having to let go of some part of ourselves. We may also feel that some sort of stigma is attached to such work, that something must be wrong with us if we have to undertake it. (Although for Jung,[4] the process of 'individuation' – the achievement of wholeness through the bridging of the conscious and unconscious – is an entirely natural process, often for those in the second half of life.)

It is for this reason that, in *The Hungry Spirit*, Charles Handy[5] calls for 'proper selfishness', of which he says that:

> The first part of a proper selfishness… is to come to terms with ourselves as we are, and to move ourselves towards what we would like to be. Only when we are comfortable in our own skins will we be of much use to anyone else.

Take stock and begin to build self-awareness

Before we can change ourselves, we have to establish where we are now, or who we are now. Whether we wish to go through a broader process of self-renewal, or develop a specific emotional capability, such as controlling our anger, it is hard to move forward until we have first established a reliable connection with ourselves. The starting point of the learning cycle, as with any change programme, is, therefore, a form of stock-taking, although in this case it is more like an inventory of our feelings.

Getting in touch with our feelings

Getting in touch with our feelings can be difficult to do. As Hendrie Weisinger says in *Emotional Intelligence At Work:*[6]

> Tuning in to our emotions is not something that comes easily to most of us. Part of the problem is that to tune into feelings – especially distressful ones such as anger, sadness, and resentment – we need to experience them, and that can be painful.

In their book *Executive EQ*, Robert Cooper and Ayman Sawaf[7] set out a number of techniques for raising and developing emotional competency in the workplace. Two that specifically relate to building self-awareness are:

- spend two or three minutes each morning sitting quietly, and just writing in a non-evaluative way about how you feel, about what's going on for you at the time
- keep a notebook with you during the day, in which you note down your reactions to the situations that occur.

Taking time out for reflection

Another technique which helps us to take stock of ourselves is to step back, literally and figuratively, from day-to-day preoccupations, whether for a few minutes, an hour, or longer. If we don't do this, there is a danger that we lose perspective – we get our noses so close to the grindstone that we cannot focus on anything else except the day-to-day getting things done. If we take time out, it gives us the opportunity to reflect and to build our self-awareness by going through a critical self-examination.

John O'Neil is a powerful advocate of retreat as a means of increasing self-knowledge. The need for a retreat may be triggered by a work crisis, burnout or just a sustained feeling of emptiness, and is a means of getting away from structured time to spend time with ourselves:

> A retreat can be any amount of time you spend away from your usual productive round of activities, as long as that time is spent in pursuit of deep learning.[8]

The deep learning is about ourselves. After the personal inventory-taking, we need to explore the inner self: 'character, history, mistakes, regrets, values, and unadmitted impulses'.[9] The intention is that self-awareness will lead to self-acceptance, which in turn will lead to a more comfortable fit between public and private personas and therefore less stress. A single retreat may not produce instantaneous results. There will undoubtedly be flashes of insight, but our self-understanding is more likely to evolve over a period of time through repetition.

Clarifying, or redefining our sense of purpose

One effective way of starting to get back in touch with ourselves as we are, rather than in one of our many roles, is to reflect on our sense of purpose. Our 'sense of purpose' is a rather grandiose way of saying what it is that we want to do with our life, our whole life, not just our work life. This does not have to result in a dramatic stretch target equivalent to Kennedy's 'put a man on the moon by the end of the decade'. It may for many of us result in an intention to continue the status quo. However, given the way in which the world is changing around us, even this will require some adaptation on our part.

One approach, used by Joanna Bisdee of Life Directions, a London-based mentoring firm, is to look back at our lives, for example at what we have achieved in each major period, and at what we have enjoyed doing, and then to look forward to what we want to achieve and what is still to do. This helps to put where we are now in perspective. It also helps us to get in touch with what is important for us, with our own value system and with how we feel about these things.

Taking stock in this way can remind us, for example, that many of the things we value most have little to do with our careers, and that the way we value them depends on how we feel about them, not on how we think about them. There may or may not be a tangible output from this process – some have found it helpful to write down, and rewrite at intervals, their values and what they hope to achieve.

One important outcome is likely to be a sense of positive self-regard, which Warren Bennis identifies as essential for a successful leader, and a feeling of potency, of being in control of our destiny, as opposed to being subject to the whim of fortune, or of others.

Set change goals

The process of taking stock helps us to confront reality and to see ourselves as we really are. This will hopefully be accompanied by self-acceptance, but it may also encourage us to identify those gaps between where we are now and where we want to be. This, in turn, gives us the basis on which to set change goals. These may be very specific, such as to increase our level of self-motivation, or more general, such as to continue to build our self-awareness.

Practice

How can you practice your emotions? Unlikely as it may seem, the boundaries of what can be achieved by practice are much broader than we might think. A study by Michael Howe,[10] a professor of psychology at Exeter University, and his colleagues into outstanding performance in sport and the arts – two areas classically considered to rely on innate talent – concludes that excellence is certainly dependant upon opportunity, encouragement, training, motivation and self-confidence, but is most of all achieved through practice.

But what do we practice when it comes to our feelings? The first thing is to increase our routine level of self-awareness by using some of the techniques referred to above, such as 'tuning in' to how we feel, maybe using quiet time for reflection, a notebook to capture our feelings as they happen, or simply sitting down at regular intervals and talking to someone, such as a counsellor or therapist, about how we feel.

The next thing we can do is focus on and manage certain behaviours which result from how we feel. Goleman[11] cites an example of one individual's plan to increase emotional self-control which consisted of a combination of learning and regularly practising control techniques, role-playing challenging situations, and asking for feedback from peers when they spotted negative behaviours.

In a general sense, we can practise our intuitive ability in our day-to-day lives by deliberately allowing ourselves to be open to what our instincts, particularly our first reactions, are telling us about a particular situation. This can be harder than it sounds, partly because those instincts – what we call 'gut feelings' – communicate to us in ways which are very different from the rational dialogue that we hold with ourselves, which we call thinking. It can also be hard to communicate them to someone else. In fact, we may have to consciously disengage our critical rational abilities – to suspend disbelief – before we can make use of all the information available to us from other means.

Ask for feedback

Although it may be difficult to ask for, it is extremely helpful to supplement our own assessment of our progress with frank feedback from those around us. This is partly because there are aspects of ourselves which, rather like the back of our head, are an essential part of who we are, but which we cannot directly see ourselves, and partly because it is natural for us to focus more on our own short-comings rather than on what we do well. Research has shown that people who are competent are more likely to underestimate that competence, whereas those who are incompetent are more likely to fail to recognise their incompetence, since it takes the same skills to recognise competence as to be competent.

As we all know, the impact of one word of criticism is greater and longer-lasting than that of a hundred words of praise. However, other people's views help to correct the balance. What is more, they often provide us with data on the positives of ourselves which we need to build on. This makes positive feedback doubly helpful – it is both information we can act on, and intrinsically motivating.

Make sure you have support throughout the process

Whether the purpose of the self-learning is to make specific changes, or simply to keep the feet firmly on the ground, it will be hard to achieve without help. The help can come at a number of points, starting with the regular critical self-evaluation, which Peter Drucker sees as one of the characteristics of effective leaders:

> They made sure that the person they saw in the mirror in the morning was the kind of person they wanted to be, respect, and believe in.[12]

We may be able to hold a mirror up to ourselves, but we assume wrongly that it gives an accurate image. We forget, for example, that it is in reverse, or we only focus on what we want to see, and choose to overlook the blemishes. It helps if there is someone else there, too, since an objective observer can draw our attention to what has become familiar, and help to interpret what we see.

This is particularly true if they bring new data, since 'feedback is the breakfast of champions'. Feedback, however, must be frank if it is to be helpful, and it is extremely hard to achieve this from within an organisation. Even though a process of encouraging peer and subordinate feedback may be in place there is pressure on us to tone down what we say for fear of how it will be received.

An outsider is more likely to be able to 'tell it as it is', or to help us to 'see it as it is', although they too will have their own ego needs, and will have to work hard to recognise, and neutralise, their own agenda for such a relationship.

We also need help to sustain our momentum in pursuing whatever goals the feedback suggests. This support takes several forms, such as providing a framework of regular meetings, holding our feet to the fire (figuratively, of course) when we stray into denial and motivating and encouraging us when we need it.

Other contributions that another person such as a coach or counsellor can make include helping us to find models, or clarifying 'what good looks like', reinforcing change as it happens by helping us to identify what has changed and providing recognition for that achievement.

The organisational dimension: an emotionally healthy culture

The challenges of creating an emotionally literate workplace are testified to by Claude Steiner in *Achieving Emotional Literacy*, who considers that the power plays, subtle and otherwise, and secrets present in most organisations can turn the workplace into 'a minefield of emotionally illiterate, toxic transactions'.[13] For Faith Ralston, in *Hidden Dynamics*, one of the biggest barriers is 'fear, a pervasive emotion in organisations today'.[14]

At the very least, a leader should care enough to prevent emotional ill health in their organisation and to create, as far as possible, a culture which recognises and manages the downsides of stress, or of dysfunctional, internal conflict. At best, a leader can create an environment in which the emotional energy is devoted to creative ends, where change is accepted readily, if not actively embraced, and the individual's need for fulfilment is met. Idealistic, perhaps, but not necessarily unrealistic.

There are a number of ways in which a leader can do this: through their own values, and the expectations and standards they set for the organisation; the manner in which they conduct themselves in their business lives; and through the policies and processes that they put in place in the organisation.

Personal value system

Since the leader is the most copied person in the organisation, their own value system will be much scrutinised. The leader's own priorities have to be seen to be in line with those they set for the organisation.

Setting expectations

The leader can establish what the values of the organisation are to be, and that means values in a day-to-day practical sense, as well as at a higher level. Stanley Davis, one of the earliest researchers into corporate culture, distinguishes between guiding beliefs and daily beliefs.[15] There is little point having lofty guiding beliefs if they do not translate into how decisions are made and how time is prioritised on a daily basis. Which company does not say, somewhere in their annual report to shareholders, that 'people are our greatest asset'? And in how many companies would those people say it feels like it?

To encourage a supportive climate, the leader can make it clear that emotional well-being is a legitimate business issue, that the organisation is mature enough to recognise its value, and that this is an area where a business case in financial terms is not needed.

How leaders conduct themselves in their business lives

The influence of personal example is extremely powerful, for good or for bad. How a leader conducts him- or herself in reality will, therefore, have the single biggest influence on whether the organisation takes the subject seriously. Characteristics which set an example of personal emotional health include appearing comfortable with the role and responsibilities, having a quality of life beyond work, taking time out to refresh, using humour, and keeping a sense of perspective.

How the leader treats those they work with

Since we tend to treat others in the way we ourselves are treated, the way in which the leader behaves towards the people he directly works with not only makes clear what his value system really is, it also passes on a code of approved behaviour. There are several behaviours which are characteristic of an emotionally literate leader:

- they make time in a busy schedule for giving and getting coaching
- they proactively invite feedback
- they relate to the non-work sides of those who work for them. For example, they take the time to learn about things such as what they do when they are not at work, their general state of health, and what is going on in their families
- they make time to be available
- they are excellent listeners
- they spend time on developing people, and encouraging learning
- they set stretch goals, but trust people to deliver, and can contain their own anxiety and refrain from interference
- they allow mistakes as long as they are seen as opportunities for learning rather than for blame
- people feel free to speak the truth
- decisions are made openly, with the involvement of those affected
- disagreement is seen not as a threat, but as a sign of health.

The HR policies and procedures they put in place

The value system of the organisation is often expressed most clearly in its formal people processes such as performance appraisal, training and development and reward. The leader has to ensure that all these policies, not just the more obvious employee welfare ones, help to create a culture which is supportive of emotional well-being. For example, some of the characteristics which make these policies truly supportive are:

■ A 360-degree performance appraisal process in which there is enough training, support and quality control to ensure that managers do step up to the hard task of giving negative feedback when needed, and in which the subordinate feels able to give the manager at least a modicum of unfiltered feedback.
■ Career development which is individual-oriented, rather than company-oriented, and held in place by effective mentoring which gives the employee alternative sources of advice, counsel and inspiration.

The quality of work life they promote

Many of the boundaries critical to emotional health are becoming very blurred, whether between home and office, between work and play, between colleagues and family, between company time and home time, or between the individual as an employee and him- or herself.

An organisation's approach to the quality of work life is critical, and, in the competition for hard-to-find and high-value-add employees, some US companies are catering for the whole self by providing a workplace which *Fortune* described as:

> Where you can eat, nap, swim, shop, pray, kick-box, drink beer, run your errands, start a romance, get your dental work done, wield plastic light sabres, and sculpt nude models.[16]

Notes

Prologue

1. Levinson, 1996 p. 158
2. John Gray, 1992
3. Tichy and Sherman, 1993 p. 64
4. Ashford and Humphrey, 1995
5. Cooper and Sawaf, 1997 p. xxxiii
6. Sir John Harvey-Jones, quoted in Sadler, 1997 p. 47

PART I

Chapter 1

1. Tichy and Sherman, 1993 p. 64
2. Bennis and Nanus, 1997
3. Dianne Hales, 1999 pp. 259ff.

Chapter 2

1. Warren Bennis, 1989 p. 1
2. Kets de Vries, 1995 p. 82
3. Van Seters and Field, 1990 summarised in Sadler, 1997 pp. 28–31
4. Bennis and Nanus, 1997
5. Kets de Vries, 1995 p. 13
6. Philip Sadler, 1997
7. Zaleznik, 1992 pp. 126–35
8. John Kotter, 1990 p. 102
9. Tichy and Devanna, 1986
10. Kets de Vries, 1995 p. 8
11. Zaleznik, 1992 pp. 126–35

Chapter 4

1. Gouillart and Kelly, 1995 pp. 6–7
2. Seltzer and Bass, 1990 pp. 693–703
3. Ashford and Humphrey, 1995 pp. 97ff.
4. Sir John Harvey-Jones, 1988 p. 129

Chapter 5

1. Daniel Goleman, 1998 pp. 33–4
2. Bass, 1990 quoted in Goleman, 1998 p. 196

3. Kets de Vries, 1995 p. xii
4. Kets de Vries, 1995 p. 12

PART III

Chapter 12

1. Warren Bennis, in Gibson, 1997 pp. 150–2
2. Philip Sadler, 1997 p. 110
3. Charles Handy, in Gibson, 1997 p. 31
4. Jack Welch, quoted in Lowe, 1998 p. 98
5. Warren Bennis, 1996 p. 160
6. Dave Ulrich, in Hesselbein et al., 1996 p. 217
7. John O'Neil, 1995 p. 21
8. Warren Bennis, 1989 p. 68
9. Manfred Kets de Vries, 1989 pp. 5ff.
10. John O'Neil, 1995 pp. 258–9
11. Eric Parsloe, 1995 p. 63

Chapter 13

1. Charles Handy, in Gibson, 1997 p. 6
2. Charles Handy, op. cit. p. 25
3. Charles Handy, op. cit. p. 27
4. Ricardo Semler, 1994 Foreword
5. Ricardo Semler, 1994 Foreword
6. Jon Ashworth, *The Times* 29.9.98 p. 21
7. Robin Dunbar, quoted in Nigel Nicholson, 1998 pp. 134–47
8. Warren Bennis, in Gibson, 1997 p. 150
9. Peter Senge, in Gibson, 1997 p. 132
10. Peter Senge, op. cit. p. 132
11. Kets de Vries, 1995 p. 96
12. Kets de Vries, 1989 p. 6
13. John O'Neil, 1995 p. 14
14. John O'Neil, 1995 pp. 28–31
15. Stephen Covey, in Gibson, 1997 p. 37
16. Charles Handy, in Gibson, 1997 p. 32
17. Geoffrey Colvin, *Fortune* 17.8.98 pp. 79–80
18. Michael Eisner, quoted in Cooper and Sawaf, 1997 p. 277
19. Oliver James, 1998 p. 7

PART IV

Chapter 14

1. Tichy and Sherman, 1993 p. 45
2. Daniel Goleman, 1998 p. 239
3. Daniel Goleman, 1998 pp. 254–5
4. Frieda Fordham, 1953 pp. 75–80
5. Charles Handy, 1997 p. 106

6. Hendrie Weisinger, 1998 p. 14
7. Robert Cooper and Ayman Sawaf, 1997 p. 16–17
8. John O'Neil, 1995 p. 166
9. John O'Neil, 1995 p. 170
10. Quoted in an article by John Clare, *Daily Telegraph* 11.9.98
11. Daniel Goleman, 1998 pp. 254–5
12. Peter Drucker, in Hesselbein et al., 1996 p. xiii
13. Claude Steiner, 1997 pp. 180ff.
14. Faith Ralston, 1995 pp. 35ff.
15. Stanley M. Davis, 1984
16. Jerry Useem, *Fortune* 10.1.00 pp. 45ff.

Bibliography

Ashforth Blake E. and Humphrey Ronald H., Emotion in the workplace: A reappraisal. *Human Relations*, 1995 **48**(2): 97ff.

Bass M.B., *Bass and Stodgill's Handbook of Leadership: Theory, Research and Applications*. New York, Free Press 1990. Cited in Goleman, 1998.

Bennis Warren, *On Becoming a Leader*. London, Hutchinson 1989.

Bennis Warren, The leader as storyteller. *Harvard Business Review*, January/February 1996.

Bennis Warren and Nanus, *Leaders*. New York, Harper Business 1997.

Cooper Robert and Sawaf Ayman, *Executive EQ*. London, Orion 1997.

Davis Stanley M., *Managing Corporate Culture*. Boston, Ballinger 1984.

Fordham Frieda, *An Introduction to Jung's Psychology*. London, Penguin 1953.

Gibson Rowan (ed.), *Rethinking The Future*. London, Nicholas Brealey 1997.

Goleman Daniel, *Emotional Intelligence*. London, Bloomsbury 1996.

Goleman Daniel, *Working With Emotional Intelligence*. London, Bloomsbury 1998.

Gouillart Francis J. and Kelly James N., *Transforming the Organisation*. New York, McGraw-Hill 1995.

Gray John, *Men are from Mars Women are from Venus*. New York, HarperCollins 1992.

Hales Dianne, *Just Like a Woman*. London, Virago 1999.

Handy Charles, *The Hungry Spirit*. London, Hutchinson 1997.

Harvey-Jones Sir John, *Making It Happen*. London, Collins 1988.

Hesselbein F., Goldsmith M. and Beckhard R., *The Leader of the Future*. San Francisco, Jossey-Bass 1996.

James Oliver, *Britain On The Couch*. London, Century Random House 1998.

Kets de Vries Manfred, Leaders who self-destruct: the causes and cures. *Organisational Dynamics*, Spring 1989 pp. 5ff.

Kets de Vries Manfred, *Life and Death in the Executive Fast Lane*. San Francisco, Jossey-Bass 1995.

Kotter John P., *A Force for Change: How Management Differs from Leadership*. New York, Free Press 1990.

Levinson Harry, The leader as analysor. *Harvard Business Review*, January/February 1996.

Lowe Janet C., *Jack Welch Speaks*. New York, John Wiley & Sons 1998.

Nicholson Nigel, How hardwired is human behaviour? *Harvard Business Review*, 1998 **78**(4): 134–7.

O'Neil John R., *The Paradox of Success*. London, McGraw-Hill 1995.

Parsloe Eric, *Coaching Mentoring and Assessing*. London, Kogan Page 1995.

Ralston Faith, *Hidden Dynamics*. New York, American Management Association 1995.

Sadler Philip, *Leadership*. London, Kogan Page 1997.

Semler Ricardo, *Maverick!* London, Arrow 1994.

Seltzer J. and Bass B.M., Transformational leadership: beyond initiation and consideration. *Journal of Management*, 1990 **16**: 693–703. Cited in Ashford and Humphrey, 1995.

Steiner Claude, *Achieving Emotional Literacy*. London, Bloomsbury 1997.

Tichy Noel M. and Devanna M.A., *The Transformational Leader*. New York, John Wiley 1986.

Tichy Noel M. and Sherman S., *Control Your Destiny Or Someone Else Will*. New York, Doubleday 1993.

Weisinger Hendrie, *Emotional Intelligence at Work*. San Francisco, Jossey-Bass 1998.

Zaleznik A., Managers and leaders: are they different? *Harvard Business Review*, March/April 1992, pp. 126–35.

Index

At Issue

| Teen Residential
| Treatment Programs

Other Books in the At Issue Series:

At Issue

Teen Residential Treatment Programs

Judeen Bartos, Book Editor

GREENHAVEN PRESS
A part of Gale, Cengage Learning

Detroit • New York • San Francisco • New Haven, Conn • Waterville, Maine • London

Elizabeth Des Chenes, *Director, Publishing Solutions*

For more information, contact:
Greenhaven Press
27500 Drake Rd.
Farmington Hills, MI 48331-3535
Or you can visit our Internet site at gale.cengage.com

For product information and technology assistance, contact us at

Gale Customer Support, 1-800-877-4253
For permission to use material from this text or product, submit all requests online at www.cengage.com/permissions

Further permissions questions can be emailed to permissionrequest@cengage.com

Articles in Greenhaven Press anthologies are often edited for length to meet page requirements. In addition, original titles of these works are changed to clearly present the main thesis and to explicitly indicate the author's opinion. Every effort is made to ensure that Greenhaven Press accurately reflects the original intent of the authors. Every effort has been made to trace the owners of copyrighted material.

Cover image © Images.com/Corbis.

LIBRARY OF CONGRESS CATALOGING-IN-PUBLICATION DATA

Teen residential treatment programs / Judeen Bartos, Book Editor..
p. cm. -- (At issue)
Includes bibliographical references and index.
ISBN 978-0-7377-6149-8 (hbk.) -- ISBN 978-0-7377-6150-4 (pbk.)
1. Juvenile delinquents--Rehabilitation--United States. 2. Juvenile detention homes--United States--Management 3. Children--Institutional care--United States--Management. I. Bartos, Judeen, editor of compilation.
RJ506.J88T4 2013
362.74--dc23
2012032616

Printed in the United States of America
1 2 3 4 5 6 7 17 16 15 14 13

Contents

Introduction

Teen residential treatment programs can be a lifeline to troubled youth who are experiencing difficulties in their lives. Some teens voluntarily seek help for issues ranging from substance abuse to depression to eating disorders. Others may be forced to attend programs, either by parents who are desperate for help with a child they feel is out of control or by the legal system when juveniles break the law. Many treatment programs do prove beneficial in assisting teens with behavioral issues and getting them on a more positive track. Others, however, may have a devastating impact on the future of the teens they serve.

Troubled teen treatment programs such as boot camps tout the use of military style discipline and hard work to achieve results. These programs guarantee dramatic behavioral changes in the youth that are consigned to them, but the reality is often far from the promise. Boot camps became popular in the 1980s and early 1990s as the supposed answer to managing troubled teens. Judges used them as an alternative for young offenders who otherwise may have been sent to adult prisons. Parents of underage youth saw them as a way of keeping their children out of the juvenile justice system and as a deterrent to getting into more serious trouble. This form of teen treatment has since fallen out of favor, as it proved to be ineffective in producing lasting change. However, these programs persist as a form of treatment in large part due to lax regulation.

Troubled teen treatment programs are often run by privately owned corporations that contract with individual state departments. Owners answer to shareholders who may be more concerned with profits and earnings than with rehabilitating troubled youth. Within this design, a lack of federal regulation has led to widespread abuse and mistreatment as operators try to run programs for the least amount of money, often cutting corners in order to improve profits. Without federal oversight, many of the worst operators simply move from state to state to avoid prosecution. States are often not financially able to oversee the programs and prosecute violations. Laws vary among states, and many state systems do not communicate with each other. Maia Szalavitz described the situation in *TIME* magazine in 2011, stating, "Nail salons and dog outfits are, in fact, more strictly regulated than troubled teen programs, which routinely use corporal punishment and isolation in the guise of treatment."

A prison in Mississippi provides an example of the dysfunction inherent in the for-profit model of delivering treatment in a poorly regulated environment. Walnut Grove Youth Correctional Facility was managed by the GEO Group, a private firm that is one of the world's largest operators of correctional facilities and other types of residential treatment centers. A federal investigation and lawsuit by the Southern Poverty Law Center were initiated against the management group after hundreds of complaints of brutality were lodged against the facility. Inadequate staffing, poor training, and rampant violence and abuse were just some of the deficiencies uncovered at Walnut Grove, described as "a cesspool of unconstitutional and inhumane acts and condition" by US District Court Judge Carlton W. Reeves in his March 26, 2012, court order issued to clean up the facility.

The environment at Walnut Grove is not an isolated instance. Private facilities funded by public tax dollars are often not held accountable for their actions, with penalties and fines woefully inadequate to force operators to improve operations or get out of the business. Indeed, the GEO Group, which has been the subject of other investigations and lawsuits, has been operating since 1988. And its facilities have proven quite profitable despite the legal actions against them—GEO Group's chief executive officer, George C. Zoley, who is also the company's founder, earned almost $6 million in salary, bonuses, and long-term compensation in 2011, according to figures reported in *Smart Money* magazine.

Booth Gunter, writing in a May 14, 2012, article for OpEdNews.com, zeroes in on the crux of the problem: "The story of Walnut Grove is a cautionary tale that calls into question the wisdom of turning over prisoners, some as young as 13, to private companies that exist solely to turn a profit. These companies have no incentive to rehabilitate offenders. Instead, they thrive on recidivism and increase their profits by cutting corners and reaping ever more troubled souls into their walls." Crucial to this discussion is the lack of motivation for for-profit treatment facilities to rehabilitate their residents. A decrease in juveniles receiving treatment should be cause for celebration, a sign that early intervention and rehabilitation methods are working. But if the goal is to make money, empty beds mean fewer profits.

Treating troubled teens, either those who are incarcerated or seeking help voluntarily, is challenging under the best circumstances. But attempting to do so and also make a profit is an especially dubious endeavor. When combined with weak laws and inadequate monitoring systems, the results can be dangerous for youth. The viewpoints in *At Issue: Teen Residential Treatment Programs* reflect this and other perspectives on this important topic.

1

Residential Treatment Centers Offer Teens Respite from Toxic Situations

Judy Battle

Judy Battle is a New Jersey writer, sociologist, and mental health and addictions specialist.

Many substance-abusing teens benefit from the structure and consistency that residential treatment programs offer. Removal from a home environment that is chaotic and exposes teens to many temptations, including substance-abusing peers, is beneficial. Good treatment centers strive to treat not only the teen's substance abuse issues but also their underlying causes—such as family relationships and low self-esteem—in order to help teens make changes that will last a lifetime.

> "It finally happened. Joan is now in a residential treatment center for her alcohol and drug problems. It was hard to send our 14-year-old daughter away but she was so out of control. Curfew meant nothing and we started noticing things missing around the house—small items like her brother's Walkman and my watch.
>
> "Last weekend, she went to a friend's birthday party and passed out from acute alcohol poisoning. We were so scared that she would die. I'm not exactly sure how this treatment facility is going to help Joan, but I know her mother and I are at our wit's end."
>
> —Mr. Robert J.—

Adolescence—even without alcohol and drug abuse—is a difficult maturational passage. It is the bridge between the dependency of childhood and adult identity. It is a time of rebellion, "trying on" adult behaviors and extensive limit testing in all areas.

Unfortunately, when alcohol and drugs are involved, many youngsters are unable to handle the physical and emotional consequences. The limits that are broken—legal and physical—often leave a teen in dangerous situations.

Residential treatment is often the last stop for an out-of-control substance-abusing teenager. It offers a "time out" from situations that trigger self-destructive behavior, a chance to experience predictable and consistent consequences of behavior, an opportunity to participate in community, and for family bonds to be repaired. In the process, self-esteem—the major antidote to alcohol and drug use—is increased.

How does this happen? Let's follow Joan J. through several aspects of her treatment experience.

Residential Treatment Creates a Space for "Time-Out"

Joan's entrance into a residential facility immediately separated her from alcohol and drugs, peers using these substances and ineffective parental rules. In their place was a world that was structured, supervised, therapeutic and substance-free.

Joan was not happy with this change. She began to experience mild to moderate withdrawal symptoms and spent her first days detoxing. When this discomfort ended she was enraged at losing her freedom.

"I hate my mother and my father for putting me here. I hate myself for getting caught and not being able to handle the booze and coke. I see the other kids here kidding around with each other and hate them too."

Her parents, hearing about the daily schedule of school, community meetings, chores and therapy sessions were sure Joan would either run away or refuse to participate. But, despite her anger, Joan did not fight the new rules.

The heart of most residential treatment programs is the "level system."

"She seems almost relieved that something bigger than her is in charge," said Mrs. J. "Maybe she is as tired of fighting as we are."

Predictable and Consistent Consequences Help Increase Responsible Behavior

The heart of most residential treatment programs is the "level system." During orientation, Joan was made aware of four stages of increasing responsibility and privileges. To advance to the next level, she had to demonstrate responsibility, self-awareness, and make a positive contribution to the general community.

She began at level one—orientation—and had no privileges. It was easy to move to level two. All she had to do was accept a job, be on time for individual and family counseling sessions, and attend community meetings, and she could leave her unit and make phone calls.

Level three required a note from her job supervisor that she was doing well, making a positive contribution to all counseling sessions, and participating in community meetings. Rewards included weekend family passes, the right to spend money at the commissary, and a one-hour-later bedtime.

The fourth level involved taking a leadership role in the community. It meant leading an orientation session for newcomers, writing out the reasons why she came to be in residential treatment and what needed to change when she got home so that she would not need additional residential treatment. The reward was to countdown the days before she could go home and enjoy a fairly nonrestrictive time on her unit.

In order to advance to a higher level, a resident had to present his case to the entire community, staff and teens. If there were negative votes, he could not advance. Each negative vote had to be explained face-to-face to the applicant.

Recovery from substance abuse requires that the chemical high be replaced by some other source of feeling good.

Like most teens, Joan would advance a level or two and then break a rule and return to level one. She was testing to see if the counselors meant what they said. Once she was finally convinced of the consistency of consequences, she advanced to the fourth level.

Joan was proud of her newly acquired leadership skills, and her parents and counselors noticed the dramatic increase in her self-esteem.

Residents Participate in Community Building

Recovery from substance abuse requires that the chemical high be replaced by some other source of feeling good. In addition, the psychological pain that is medicated by alcohol and other drugs must be faced therapeutically and healed.

"I'm learning about natural highs," says Joan. "This morning we did this really neat trust exercise where we each took turns climbing a platform and falling backwards into the arms of the entire group. The first time I did it I was really scared they would drop me. But they didn't. And the second time I just shut my eyes and loved it!"

Joan also spends time daily with her counselor identifying and talking about her feelings. She is beginning to talk about how afraid she is that her parents will divorce and that no boy will ever want to date her. She loves to write in her journal and draws pictures of a little girl who used to be sad but is starting to smile.

Family Bonds Are Repaired Before Returning Home

Before a youth can go home, the bonds between parent and child so severely strained during the height of teen alcohol and drug abuse need to be repaired. This is accomplished through the involvement of family members in the treatment process.

Studies consistently show that treating alcohol and drug abuse in teens is a wise investment.

Family therapy sessions are held on a regular basis. Feelings of anger, fear, shame and love are expressed. Strategies for conflict resolution are developed. The rules of the home are stated and clear consequences for violation outlined. A reward system is developed for good behavior. Finally, a list of therapeutic resources is drawn up in case a third party is needed for mediation.

Some facilities have an evening or a day designated as Family Day. It is a time of sharing of food, watching an educational presentation and discussing how this lesson applies to the family unit. Topics may cover the nature of addiction, self-help groups, or how families resolve conflicts.

Joan's father summed it up nicely:

"I am so happy that we found help for Joan but in reality our whole family has been positively affected by her treatment. We talk to one another and are learning to listen. Both my wife and I have decided to enter individual therapy to address our own issues. If Joan can risk growing, we can, too."

Studies consistently show that treating alcohol and drug abuse in teens is a wise investment. Not only is heavy drinking and drug use diminished but adolescents receiving treatment have fewer thoughts of suicide, lower hostility and higher self-esteem. They also report better-than-average grades.

2

Teens in Residential Programs Are Treated Like Terrorists

Maia Szalavitz

Maia Szalavitz is a journalist who covers health, science, and public policy. Szalavitz's work has been published in TIME, *the* New York Times, Elle, Scientific American Mind, *the* Washington Post, New Scientist, *and* Psychology Today. *She is also the author of* Help at Any Cost: How the Troubled-Teen Industry Cons Parents and Hurts Kids.

The similarities between the treatment of teens in "tough love" camps and captured terrorists are startling. Isolation, deprivation, and humiliation are employed in both cases, and Americans seem to be ambivalent about the cruelty inflicted on both groups. In the case of terrorists, it is assumed that these techniques will lead to a captive revealing information that may prevent future acts of terror. In the case of teens in a treatment center, there is the belief that all these kids need to straighten up is some discipline and rigor. The types of psychological and physical torture used in both cases does not result in any real success and instead causes lasting damage to both victims and perpetrators.

We are, famously, blasé about our acts of torture overseas. But why? The laser-like focus on fixing the economy, wanting to avoid more political divisiveness, the diminishment of watchdog journalism—are all part of the explanation. But there's another overlooked reason as well.

Americans tend to valorize tough love—at times, even tough love that verges on torture—in prisons, mental hospitals, drug rehabs, and teen boot camps. We aren't squeamish about the psychological aspects of torture. We might even admire them.

Thousands of troubled children, for instance, now attend tough "wilderness programs," "emotional growth boarding schools" and other "tough love" camps where they face conditions like total isolation, sleep deprivation, food deprivation, and daily emotional attacks.

If more people understood the psychological and physical consequences of these "thought reform" techniques, I don't think we'd find them acceptable for anyone.

Thousands also attend religiously based residential programs, some of which claim to "cure" homosexuality and stop teen promiscuity. In this context, the recent poll showing that evangelicals are the group with the highest level of support for torture begins to make sense.

Troubled Teens Subjected to Same Tactics Used on Al-Qaeda Prisoners

If we think humiliation, stress positions, and isolation are OK for disobedient teens, why not for suspected terrorists?

As the author of the first book-length history and expose of the troubled-teen industry, I'm familiar not only with the distressing stories of abuse coming from these programs, but also with their roots in the same tactics now being exposed in the CIA [US Central Intelligence Agency] torture program.

If more people understood the psychological and physical consequences of these "thought reform" techniques, I don't think we'd find them acceptable for anyone.

Here's what is known about the parallels between "enhanced interrogation" teen boot camps and the idea of "thought reform" programs first described by psychiatrist Robert J. Lifton in the 1950's—and about how they damage the mind and body.

As we've learned from the torture memos, the tactics used against suspected [terrorist group] Al-Qaeda prisoners were based on American military counter-interrogation training known as SERE (Survival, Evasion, Resistance and Escape). SERE tried to teach soldiers to resist tactics that were used by the Chinese and Koreans in the 1950's to break American servicemen and their own citizens.

Humiliating Regimens Lead to Traumatic Outcomes

Breaking someone, it turns out, needn't involve much of what conventionally has been called torture. Instead, by the skillful control of the environment and use of things like complete isolation from the outside world, stress positions, hard physical labor, sleep deprivation, food deprivation, temperature extremes and humiliation, one can create a regime that relatively quickly warps the mind and produces at least the illusion of compliance.

All of these tactics—everything short of water-boarding—have been found to be used in a surprising number of teen programs. In 1974, in fact, a Congressional investigation said that tactics used by The Seed program on kids were "similar to the highly refined brainwashing techniques employed by the North Koreans in the early 1950's."

Hundreds of programs operating now are directly or indirectly tied to the program that was the model for The Seed, a cult called Synanon.

In an October 2007 Congressional hearing, Government Accountability Office investigators and other witnesses described teens being publicly humiliated, sleep deprived, starved, denied medical care and "forced to eat vomit [and] lie in urine and feces." So this has been done to kids for at least three decades.

The key to understanding why these controlling, humiliating regimens work to produce apparent compliance and how dangerous they are to mental health is social neuroscience. It turns out that the human stress system is modulated by social support. That means that what turns off—or on—our stress systems, is mainly other people.

In fact, keeping one's stress hormones balanced requires the comfort of others: Even short periods of forced isolation can make them spiral out of control.

The more helpless a person feels, the more dangerous traumatic stress becomes.

If in addition, you deprive someone of all physical affection, further overload the stress system via temperature extremes, low calorie diets, and physical stresses like over-exercise or confinement, you have a perfect storm of traumatic experience.

A Sense of Control Is Taken Away from Teens in Programs

A critical element here is combining these tactics to undermine any sense of control—the more helpless a person feels, the more dangerous traumatic stress becomes. The psychologists who devised the "enhanced interrogation techniques" explicitly wanted to create dependence, reading the literature on what psychologist Martin Seligman termed "learned helplessness."

Learned helplessness is actually based on an animal model of depression, and has also been linked with causing PTSD [post traumatic stress disorder], panic attacks, and even reduced immunity.

Another aspect that interrogators recognize to be critical in destroying a person's sense of self is humiliation. This includes seemingly benign things like taking away preferred clothing and more extreme identity degradation tactics like keeping people either naked or in humiliating outfits and denying bathroom access, including hygiene.

Constant emotional attacks—particularly sexual humiliation and insults that emphasize worthlessness and hopelessness—also help leave people vulnerable to the provision of brief moments of kindness, for which, by that point, most people will do or say anything.

Chronic, Intense Stress Can Damage Areas of the Brain

It seems hard to believe that it is that easy to break people's wills—but understanding the brain's stress system again offers insight. Under intense stress, higher brain regions have less control over the mind and body: the faster, more reactive regions dominate in order to facilitate fight or flight.

This literally makes us less intelligent and more pliable—and that makes evolutionary sense. Early humans who were contemplative during emergencies probably left fewer descendants.

Damaging the brain regions responsible for concentration and memory and potentially inducing psychotic delusions is not a good way to discover the truth or promote better behavior.

And chronic, intense stress can be even more damaging: it "burns in" these hair-trigger responses and connections that give greater control to lower brain regions while damaging the area needed for long-term learning and memory, the hippocampus. This can produce depression, post-traumatic stress disorder, and even high blood pressure, heart disease, and stroke.

However, because of social modulation of stress and the importance of a sense of control, these conditions do not have anywhere near as great an impact if the person chooses voluntarily to undergo them, has social support and knows that the ordeal will end at a certain time.

Comparing a teen who chooses to stay up all night partying or a guy who likes to stand while working at the office with people who are forced to do those things is thus invalid. The physiology of voluntarily undergoing time-limited stress induced by people you trust and being forced into it by those you don't are completely different.

Despite Severity of Tactics, Tough Love Programs Rarely Lead to Lasting Change

There would be an interesting debate to be had on the use of these regimes if they produced lasting positive behavior change in the direction desired by their enforcers. In terms of interrogation, some people might find it acceptable to intentionally provoke depression and PTSD in suspected terrorists if that could prevent attacks. In terms of addicts and teenagers, however, it makes no sense at all, given that both PTSD and depression increase the risk of developing new addictions or relapse to older ones.

And, in fact, imposing traumatic stresses—as the researchers who studied the victims of the Koreans and the Chinese discovered back in the 1950's and 60's—is not a good way of producing either reliable information or behavior change. Damaging the brain regions responsible for concentration and memory and potentially inducing psychotic delusions is not a good way to discover the truth or promote better behavior.

Stories of teens held in abusive drug programs are instructive here: there are countless cases of false confessions. Kids who had done nothing more than smoke pot came out with tales of shooting heroin and smoking crack—virgins told stories of becoming prostitutes forced to have sex with animals in order to support their habits. These were not isolated events—having interviewed dozens of kids with this experience, false confessions were a common thread, many of them bizarre. Drug-related behavior after the program was often far worse than before.

The data on both teen treatment and legal interrogations by the FBI are clear: torturous tactics are both unnecessary and harmful.

Everyone Suffers Under Abusive Conditions

Further, while many people are resilient to traumatic stress and some are made stronger by it, the damage done by imposing it doesn't just affect victims. Perpetrators are harmed, too—by feelings of guilt, by having to shut off compassion and empathy and by the corrupting nature of having absolute power over people.

This also produces an acceptance of the previously unacceptable, a culture of callousness that erodes trust and replicates itself, causing more hopelessness and calls for even more extreme measures.

If we want to return to America's ideals, we have to look at why we've tolerated this kind of treatment for anyone—not just terrorists, but vulnerable youth—for decades.

Most of all, we need to stop thinking that getting tough is the answer to everything. It's often harder to resist kindness and compassion than it is to submit to brute force and tell your captors what you think they want to hear. This is, in part, why the FBI [US Federal Bureau of Investigation] wanted nothing to do with "enhanced interrogation." The data on both teen treatment and legal interrogations by the FBI are clear: torturous tactics are both unnecessary and harmful.

By eliminating these coercive regimes from every aspect of our culture, we will not only do good, but do well.

3

Former Students Sue Troubled-Teen Institutions for Abuse

Jennifer Dobner

Jennifer Dobner is a journalist in Salt Lake City, Utah. Dobner previously worked as an Associated Press reporter for seven years.

Former students, who claim their treatment at private residential centers was inhumane and abusive, are suing the World Wide Association of Specialty Programs and Schools (WWASPS). The allegations are widespread and involve students from thirty-eight states, Canada, and England who attended WWASPS schools. Also troubling is the lack of oversight that allowed the organization to stay in business by repeatedly closing and opening schools in different locations.

A Utah company that ran a network of domestic and international schools for troubled teens is being sued by more than 350 former students who claim they were denied food and medical care, lived in filth and suffered extreme physical and sexual abuse.

"Such abuses were inflicted on some children for several years," the lawsuit states. "In many instances, the abuse could be accurately described as torture of children."

Among the abuses detailed in the lawsuit include being exposed to extreme hot or cold temperatures for extended periods; being forced to eat raw or rotten foods or to eat their own vomit; being bound by the hands and feet; and being placed in isolation, including being locked inside small boxes or cages.

Some students also allege they were emotionally and verbally abused, were forced to wear unwashed clothing for weeks, were prevented from using bathrooms, were deprived of sleep and were deprived of any religious affiliations other than Mormonism.

The lawsuit was filed on behalf of more than 350 former students and 150 of their parents in Salt Lake City's 3rd District Court last week. The students are from 38 states, England and Canada and attended the residential school programs between the mid-1990s and mid-2000s.

The lawsuit alleges fraud, breach of contract and abuse by the World Wide Association of Specialty Programs and Schools and its affiliates and seeks a jury and unspecified damages.

Named as defendants in the lawsuit are the World Wide Association of Specialty Programs and Schools and its three principals, Robert B. Lichfield of Toquerville, and Brent M. Facer and Ken Kay, both of St. George.

Also named are a network of nearly 50 other affiliated businesses and individuals, which the lawsuit claims were also controlled by the organization's principals through either family relationships or written management agreements.

No hearings have been set in the case, and it was not immediately clear whether any of the 54 defendants were represented by attorneys.

The lawsuit alleges fraud, breach of contract and abuse by the World Wide Association of Specialty Programs and Schools and its affiliates and seeks a jury and unspecified damages. The suit renews claims in a 2006 lawsuit filed in Salt Lake City's U.S. District Court that was dismissed by a judge for jurisdictional reasons in August [2011].

The attorneys who represented the schools, Lichfield, Facer and Kay in that lawsuit did not immediately respond to telephone and email messages Thursday [September 2011].

New schools were continually created to take in students from schools that were abruptly shut down.

In court papers, attorneys for the students say World Wide has operated more than 20 schools in seven states and in Costa Rica, Jamaica, Mexico, Samoa and the Czech Republic, although the exact number and how many remain in operation is unclear.

Many of the schools were open for only short periods because of their failure to comply with licensing and regulatory laws, because of abuse allegations, and because the organization's "principals drained excessive funds off the top," court papers allege.

New schools were continually created to take in students from schools that were abruptly shut down. But the directors and staff at the new schools were often "the same incompetent and untrained" people who ran the schools that had been closed.

The students' attorneys say World Wide charged families thousands in monthly tuition, but then failed to provide adequate education or therapeutic treatment programs.

Windle Turley, a Dallas [Texas]-based attorney representing the families, says state and local authorities in some places have moved to shut down or investigate the schools. In New York, the attorney general's office conducted a criminal investigation of a school near the U.S.-Canada border. Authorities in Costa Rica and Mexico also have conducted probes, Turley said.

The New York case resulted in a 2005 settlement and the school was ordered to partially reimburse tuition costs to parents and stop advertising that it offered educational diplomas because it was not recognized by the state as an accredited school, the *Deseret News* of Salt Lake City has reported.

State attorneys also said the school, Ivy Ridge, was behind one of the largest education fraud cases in New York's history.

The newspaper also reports that Mexican officials raided and shut down a school called Casa by the Sea in 2004.

In June, an individual student who claims he attended Casa by the Sea filed a separate federal lawsuit against World Wide and its owners.

Carl Brown Austin, 24, of Spokane [Washington], claims he spent nearly two years in the Ensenada, Mexico, school and was a "virtual prisoner" in programs that meted out primitive punishment for hours on end.

When Austin's lawsuit was filed, Facer told the Associated Press he had served on World Wide's board, but that the organization had shut down because there was no longer a need for its programs.

Asked why former students might bring such accusations, Facer said children brought to such schools have a history of misrepresenting the truth.

"That's why these kids need help," Facer said. "They lie to their parents, lie to their superiors, teachers, people who maybe they would consider an authoritative type of figure. That's not uncommon."

4

Christian Boarding Schools Have a History of Abusing Young Residents

Andy Kopsa

Andy Kopsa is a journalist and blogger who writes about politics, equality, and religion.

The institutions founded by Jack Patterson are just the latest in a long line of Christian boarding schools to be accused of child abuse. Former victims provide a glimpse into the horrors that they and many others endured at schools that hide behind the cover of Christianity while administering harsh and inhumane treatment. That these schools are allowed to move from state to state with no governmental oversight is the sin, not the behavior of the so-called wayward youth who attend the schools.

Dr. Jack Patterson, founder of the Christian boarding school, Reclamation Ranch, goes on trial for aggravated child abuse March 10, 2010, in Blount County, Alabama. The trial comes two years after a 17-year-old male resident came forward with charges of severe abuse, torture and beating.

"The search by law enforcement and the questioning of involved minors yielded corroboration of the original allegations and evidence of other instances of mistreatment," said Blount County District Attorney Tommy Rountree, in a *Birmingham News* article. One report said investigators seized handcuffs and shackles from the facility, and as the clip mentions, handguns and rifles were also present.

Eleven juvenile boys were sent home from Reclamation Ranch pending the outcome of the investigation. Jack Patterson was at the courthouse in November 2008 when Alabama Circuit Court Judge Steve King made the ruling. He wasn't alone—about 200 of his supporters came out that day. A handful of those gathered, according to the *Birmingham News*, blew Dr. Jack kisses as he looked down from a second story window.

Patterson offered no comment except to say, "God bless you."

Following a Long Tradition

Dr. Jack Patterson is not a doctor. He received an honorary title from the Pacific Garden Mission Institute. Patterson holds a Bachelor's Degree in Religious Education from Hyles Anderson College—an Evangelical Christian college that spurns regulation and accreditation—in Indiana.

According to Patterson's biography posted on Reclamation Ranch's web page, he grew up in the projects of Detroit [Michigan]. After being embroiled in a life of crime and drugs, Jack found Jesus in Pensacola, Florida. From there, he entered Bible college and became a devout follower of a notorious Texas evangelist named Lester Roloff. It is important to know who Lester Roloff is, the history of his Roloff Homes, and why Patterson's stalwart allegiance to him is significant when considering these recent claims of child abuse.

Lester Roloff was the founder of "The Roloff Homes," a collection of children's reformatories that uses God and a fundamentalist form of the Baptist religion as justification for corporal punishment. He is held up today by some as a savior. But to others, he will forever be an opportunistic zealot who used his "schools" to institutionalize child abuse and warp people's ideas about what God requires of His faithful.

Roloff got his start in Texas when called to preach the good word in 1932. Roloff was just 18, living on his family's farm when he struck out pastoring at small town Baptist Churches. He caused a stir; people began to take notice. Looking for bigger and better audiences, Roloff moved to Corpus Christi and struck out in radio. His program "Family Altar" aired during World War II. As more and more listeners tuned in and "Family Altar" was picked up by KWBU—a station owned by The Baptist General Convention of Texas—Roloff decided to take his show on the road. He toured in his "gospel van" using loudspeakers to blast sermons along the way. He traveled around Texas pitching his tent, raising crowds to listen to his special brand of preaching. This was the beginning of Roloff Evangelistic Enterprises.

Roloff began criticizing mainstream Baptist counterparts on air, claiming he was the only one preaching the "*true Gospel*". His relationship with the mainstream by comparison Texas Baptist Convention ended in 1956, but his audience of followers grew and grew. Brother Roloff was nothing if not a savvy entrepreneur. He realized there was a ton of money to be made in the business of preaching. In an effort to grow his burgeoning empire, he founded The Roloff Homes, actively fundraising from his followers, calling on them to dig deep so he could do God's work.

Founder of the Rebekah Home Defends His Methods

In 1973, Roloff's the Rebekah Home was investigated by authorities for suspected abuse after a visiting couple saw a young girl being whipped. When welfare workers showed up to inspect the home, Roloff refused them entry, saying it infringed on the separation of church and state. Fortunately, Texas Attorney General John Hill didn't share that view and filed suit against Roloff Evangelistic Enterprises.

Eventually, 16 girls would come forward and tell of whippings, imprisonment, and being handcuffed to drainpipes at the hands of Rebekah Home staff. Lester Roloff defended these methods as solidly rooted in scripture. Of the charges pending against his abusive methods, Roloff said, "*Better a pink bottom than a black soul.*" Attorney General Hill said it wasn't pink bottoms he objected to but ones that were *black, blue and bloody.* (*Texas Monthly*)

This position of resisting governmental oversight is held to this day by many fundamentalist Christian educational organizations, schools and colleges.

In the end, the Rebekah House closed, [but] not because of a conviction of Roloff or his staff for repeated abuses. Facing more legal battles with the state of Texas over the newly adopted Child Care Licensing Act, Roloff, in what became known as "The Christian Alamo," shut the place down. Roloff didn't care for the notion of Christians needing the Government to give them the seal of approval saying, "*I have no right to go by the Welfare Department's little brown book so long as I have the big black Book.*"

Reclamation Ranch and Others Not Officially Licensed

This position of resisting governmental oversight is held to this day by many fundamentalist Christian educational organizations, schools and colleges. Among the colleges that scoff at official licensing is Hyles Anderson College—where Jack Patterson received his degree. Reclamation Ranch is not subject to state supervision in Alabama. Neither is the school accredited by the Southern Association of Colleges and Schools (SACS) or an alternative credentialing entity called the Alabama Independent School Association.

The Lighthouse Academy, another Roloff Home, was unlicensed as well. That is where Jack Patterson came to work for Lester Roloff for three years. . . .

Like Jack Patterson, Olen King and Mack Ford are former employees and passionate followers of Lester Roloff. The New Bethany Home for Boys and Girls was a product of the Roloff legacy and it has a long history of abuse and run-ins with state and local officials. There are scores of reports of torture and abuse coming out of New Bethany, which is now officially closed. Olen King and Mack Ford were the director and founder of New Bethany School, respectfully.

Former Residents Share Their Memories of Torture

Teresa Frye, now a 42-year-old mother of four, is a survivor of the New Bethany Home in Arcadia, Louisiana. "It took me 20 years to start talking [about New Bethany] and when I found the message board, I realized what I had been remembering was real."

Teresa and her friends talk on the message board about their "who had the reddest and blackest butt" contests back in the day.

The survivor websites—Teresa's "message board"—are posted to regularly by former residents of New Bethany and practically every account reads the same: memories of torture, abuse and demoralization at the hands of Mack Ford, Olen King and other New Bethany staff. There are harrowing stories of kids that managed to run away from New Bethany like the one by James, escaping through a Louisiana swamp, and the horrifying account of a young man named Guy beaten severely with a golf club.

Teresa was raised in what she refers to as a strict, fundamentalist Baptist church, with "*red-faced preachers, hellfire and brimstone*," but Teresa says New Bethany was one-hundred times worse.

Before she was sent to New Bethany Teresa remembers Mack Ford and his girls choir performed at her family church. "They were a choir of angels to me, the girls' testimony was so uplifting, I don't know how to describe it," said Frye of her first encounter with Mack Ford, years before she would become a resident at his New Bethany School. A traveling girls choir is nothing new in the Fundamentalist arsenal. Lester Roloff devised a handpicked and disciplined girls' choir as a fundraising and recruiting tool for his original homes.

In addition to singing, the girls gave testimonies—often coached—of their salvation for the hard sell. "They were once drug users and bad kids and going wrong—but they said New Bethany and Mack Ford saved them, we all believed them." Teresa told me this, trying to help me understand how parents could possibly have been fooled and why her parents had no idea what they were sending her into. "Everything looked so good on the outside." Teresa and her friends talk on the message board about their "who had the reddest and blackest butt" contests back in the day.

Cathy "Cat" Givens, another New Bethany survivor, shares her experience in an email to me. Cat was at New Bethany from March through December of 1974 during which time she experienced and witnessed her share of abuse. She had her mouth stuffed with soap, accused of lying by Brother Mack Ford, to the point of vomiting. Sick to her stomach, she was then forced to eat dinner—she did so for fear of what may happen if she didn't. Cathy, her gut and mouth still full of soap couldn't help but throw up her meal. For this offense, she was switched on the calves as punishment. This is just one of several humiliations Ms. Givens endured and observed during her time at the home.

Christian Homes Repeatedly Move to Avoid Legal Action

After being forced out of Louisiana by state officials demanding New Bethany allow an inspection and get licensed, it relocated to Walterboro, South Carolina. Olen King reopened the school and shortly after, stories of abuse began to trickle out. . . .

Olen King has moved again and is reportedly operating an unlicensed, unregulated "Ranch" in North Carolina. The King Family Ministries boarding school is located in Danbury, North Carolina and is nicknamed the Second Chance Boys Ranch. Second Chance Boys Ranch is currently one of The Houston Road Baptist Church in Troutman, NC missions it supports through parishioners donations. Last fall, I was able to get King on the phone. I asked him about the current operation of his home. King claimed it was closed down—that he had cancer and there was no more boys home. I had heard this rumor before through the survivors. King abruptly hung up the phone as I attempted to get more information. I called back and the phone just rang and rang.

Jack Patterson has no known history with The New Bethany School in either Louisiana or in South Carolina, so they are isolated incidents in that sense. However, they share a common ancestor, employer and teacher they revered, Lester Roloff.

Faith-Based Governmental Programs Welcome Roloff and His Sympathizers

In 1997, then Texas Governor George W. Bush invited Lester Roloff inspired homes back with open arms and money from his newly founded "Charitable Choice" program, a state level test drive for what would become *President* Bush's nationalized Faith Based Initiative. Roloff relocated Rebekah House—after the Christian Alamo—to Missouri to escape any further child abuse investigations or state regulation (Jack Patterson has moved Reclamation Ranch, in one incarnation or another, from Indiana to Washington and finally Alabama). The director of Roloff homes convinced Governor Bush's newly established Faith-Based Task Force to recommend changes in state regulation of faith-based children's homes and child care facilities.

Homes like Mack Ford and Olen King's New Bethany Home and Lester Roloff's Rebekah Home still exist throughout the country today.

The FBO [Faith-Based Organization] Task Force was already populated with Roloff sympathizers, representatives of faith-based chemical dependency facilities who were publicly vocal in their opposition to state licensing. As a result, an alternative credentialing program called the Texas Association of Christian Child-Care Agencies (TACCCA) was born. The TACCCA was a case of the inmates running the asylum. Among its board members was the director of Teen Challenge of South Texas, an organization that was already facing reprimand for non-compliance with state health and fire codes. . . .

According to an in-depth case study on the FBO initiative in Texas, by the Rockefeller Institute of Government, supported by the Pew Charitable Trusts:

"The first agency accredited under the alternative credentialing program was the Roloff Homes. Prior to this, in a suit brought by Roloff Homes, the U.S. Supreme Court ruled that the Homes must either be licensed by the state or shut down. Rather than submitting to state licensing requirements, in 1985 the Roloff Homes relocated to Missouri. In 1997, after the Alternative Credentialing bill passed, and at Governor Bush's invitation to return to Texas and take advantage of the new changes in state law, Roloff Homes returned to the state. TACCCA re-accredited the Homes, which came to operate five facilities in the state. In spring 2000, the Texas Department of Protective and Regulatory Services (TDPRS) received complaints of physical abuse at several of the Roloff Homes facilities and pursued criminal charges. In June 2001, administrators of the Roloff Homes were found guilty of juvenile abuse in a criminal trial. By that time, the Roloff Homes had moved again to another state.". . .

Whether or not Jack Patterson has broken away from the long and continuing history of the abusive Roloff Homes and subsequent Roloff-like offshoots remains to be seen. And, if Mr. Patterson is guilty of aggravated child abuse is a matter for the Blount County court to decide. What is apparent is that homes like Mack Ford and Olen King's New Bethany Home and Lester Roloff's Rebekah Home still exist throughout the country today. A 30-second Google search will yield scores of survivor's boards, informational sites and organizations dedicated to exposing the world of people who beat kids in the name of God to turn a handsome profit.

5

US Parents Should Be Wary of Off-shore Residential Treatment Centers

Adam Williams

Adam Williams is a reporter for the Tico Times *and also writes for* Bloomberg Business Week *on topics pertaining to Costa Rica.*

The World Wide Association of Specialty Programs and Schools (WWASPS), a network of teen behavioral treatment centers, has a long history of abusive treatment of teens. One of the company's facilities in Costa Rica, a behavioral modification center known as Teen Mentor, was shut down after allegations of abuse— making it one of at least sixteen programs operated by WWASPS to be shut down in recent years. While parents feel they were tricked and lied to about how their troubled teens would be treated, some employees blame the children themselves. They claim that the difficult teens are good at manipulating their parents, and that the programs were actually helpful. WWASPS employs an intense Internet marketing program to recruit families to its centers.

Teen Mentor, a behavioral modification center that officials from the Child Welfare Office (PANI) closed March 18, is under fire by a group of parents whose children attended the program. Some former staff members, however, defend the now-defunct center.

Many parents of U.S. teens who attended the center, which was located in the Hotel Carara in the Pacific coastal town of Tárcoles, in Puntarenas [Costa Rica], say they now feel they were tricked during the program's admissions process, and that some information they were told by program administrators appears to be either erroneous or false.

A network known as the World Wide Association of Specialty Programs and Schools (WWASPS) operated Teen Mentor. In the last 15 years, at least 16 programs operated by WWASPS have been closed due to allegations of abuse or lack of operating licenses.

Shelley Sylvester, who had to make an emergency flight to Costa Rica last week to retrieve her 16-year-old son after the program was closed, says she was told that her son, who had been struggling academically and behaviorally, would be in good hands with the staff of Teen Mentor.

Some residents told welfare officers that they had witnessed or experienced abuse during the program.

"I was duped," she said. "I was at the end of my rope with my son and someone was telling me that they could help me out. They said he would receive therapy, go to class six to seven hours a day, participate in yoga, go to the beach and work out his issues. I believed it. I'm ashamed to know that there are people out there that would take advantage of struggling parents. I'm ashamed at myself for believing them."

According to Jorge Urbina, PANI's technical director, a psychologist who visited and worked with the teenagers in the program sent a report to PANI that warned of abusive practices against residents of the facility. Urbina and other PANI officials then visited the program on March 18 [2011] to investigate. When they arrived, they found no administrative staff to supervise the 20 U.S. teenagers participating in the program.

Also, some residents told welfare officers that they had witnessed or experienced abuse during the program.

"We intervened and interviewed all the kids from the program. Their reports were similar to the reports made by the psychologists about mistreatment and rights violations," Urbina told the *Tico Times*. "It was apparent that the regimen of discipline included physical, psychological and verbal mistreatment."

Urbina also said the program was not licensed to operate by the Health Ministry or PANI, which was another reason for closing it.

Some of these kids are trying to manipulate their parents by telling them false accounts of what happened.

Removal of Students Proves Controversial

PANI officials removed the teenagers from the hotel and contacted their parents via the U.S. Embassy. Several parents said they received urgent phone calls from embassy or State Department staff requesting they make emergency travel arrangements to Costa Rica to pick up their kids.

Brande Ridd, an independent contractor with the WWASPS organization and who worked at Teen Mentor for two months, said the allegations against the program "are not correct," and that she felt the majority of the parents and residents had positive experiences with the program.

"I know the facts and I know that it was a really, really good program," Ridd said. "These kids are difficult kids. They have pushed their parents to a limit and they need help, they need an intervention. They beg to go into these programs. . . . I know that the people who ran this school are very kind and very loving. But I also know that some of these kids are trying to manipulate their parents by telling them false accounts of what happened."

According to Ridd, residents were making progress in the program before PANI intervened. She said that many of the residents and parents were disappointed with the closure of the program and have already expressed plans to enter their children into WWASPS facilities at other locations.

She also said the psychologist filed the complaint while the primary administrator of Teen Mentor, Robert Walter Lichfield, was out of the country visiting his family in the U.S.

"PANI took over and made everything into disarray. They didn't ask questions, they didn't give anybody an opportunity to get to the bottom of anything," Ridd said. "It caused a lot of turmoil with all of these families. Some of them had to pay a minimum of a few thousand dollars to fly to Costa Rica and get them. Several of the kids and parents were angry. Kids were saying, 'There was no abuse. We were doing good.' Several parents were angry with how PANI handled their kids."

The case is currently being investigated by the Judicial Investigation Police (OIJ).

Since opening the first program in the 1990s, at least 16 worldwide residential programs operated by WWASPS have been closed.

Lawsuits Plague Programs in Several Locations

The Teen Mentor program is the second WWASPS program closed in Costa Rica in the last eight years.

In 2002, Narvin Lichfield, Robert's uncle, was director of the Dundee Ranch Academy in the town of Hidalgo, Orotina, west of San José. A *Tico Times* investigation that year found that many of the students who attended the academy accused Dundee staff of physical and psychological abuse.

In an interview with the *Tico Times* in 2002, Narvin explained his "high impact" behavioral modification methods, which included tactics such as making students walk 100 miles around a track under the hot Pacific sun to earn their "freedom," or forcing them to spend up to five days in "solitary confinement" as punishment for looking out of the window during a lesson.

In 2003, Dundee Ranch was closed when PANI officials raided the facility after a U.S. woman living in Costa Rica, Susan Flowers, reported to PANI that her daughter was being held against her will at the academy. The raid resulted in a student riot and 35 teens escaped from the site.

WWASPS was founded by Narvin Lichfield's brother, Robert Browning Lichfield, who is the father of Teen Mentor operator Robert Walter Lichfield.

Since opening the first program in the 1990s, at least 16 worldwide residential programs operated by WWASPS have been closed. According to documentation in a pending civil lawsuit against WWASPS in the state of Utah, "no WWASPS facility has ever been licensed by any state regulatory authority as a 'treatment center.'"

The lawsuit was filed by Dallas [Texas]-based Turley Law Firm and Salt Lake City, Utah's Parker & McConkie, both in the U.S. Court filings shows that 353 plaintiffs joined the suit against WWASPS. The civil lawsuit accuses WWASPS organization of negligence, fraud, breach of contract, battery, assault, false imprisonment and a host of other charges.

Parents say visibility and a strong Internet presence have led them to WWASPS programs for years.

WWASPS Programs Dominate Internet Advertising

Of the thousands of parents who sent their children to WWASPS-run programs, many say they found the centers online, thanks to high visibility advertising. A Google search this week of the words "Teen Mentor Costa Rica" turns up 40 results. The first six link to WWASPS-operated programs. Each website has a different domain name and provides a different contact phone number, although the sites have nearly identical home pages and graphic images, as well as matching promises of therapy at a low-cost.

Veronica Barger, whose 17-year old son was at Teen Mentor for three weeks prior to its closure, told the *Tico Times* that she looked up residential programs and teen behavioral centers online and found WWASPS programs "nearly everywhere I looked." After communicating with representatives of the program for several weeks, Barger said she was convinced the program was right for her son.

"They told me they would do everything in their power to help him," Barger said. "They said Costa Rica was beautiful, that the kids would be raising local sea turtles, that [my son] would be involved in extracurricular activities and that the program was a good fit for him. It all sounded so good. I put my confidence in them, even started a friendship with the woman that helped me. I trusted them."

Parents say visibility and a strong Internet presence have led them to WWASPS programs for years.

"I sent my daughter to a WWASPS program in 1999 at a time when the Internet was still very young," said Sue Scheff, who says that her daughter was abused at a WWASPS program in 2000. "Around that time, it seemed like everything you typed [online] about residential programs or teen help, [WWASPS] would come up in every search. It was a great marketing technique. It's scary to think that it is still working."

Yet despite the allegations of mistreatment in WWASPS programs, Ridd claims the organization isn't deserving of its bad publicity.

"There are parents out there that didn't get it their way when their child was in program and they have made it their mission to destroy WWASPS," she said. "There are thousands of kids and parents that are so thankful for what the program did for them. It forever benefitted their lives."

6

Proposed Legislation to Regulate Teen Programs Is Unlikely to Prevent Abuse

Marcus Chatfield

Marcus Chatfield is a guitar-maker who lives in Asheville, North Carolina. He is a survivor of Straight Inc., a privately operated franchise of federally funded behavior modification facilities that was endorsed by the White House for two decades.

While there has been legislation proposed to regulate the actions of the troubled-teen industry, nothing to date in the United States has been done to enforce standards and prevent abuse in these private programs. Given the long-term relationships between this industry and various governmental programs it seems unlikely that an inherently flawed system will change no matter how many laws are passed. The only hope for true reform is through increased public awareness and education regarding the lasting damage to teens these programs can cause.

I called Congressman George Miller's office to ask about his proposed legislation which aims to prevent abuse and deaths within America's adolescent residential treatment programs. They told me there are no efficacy standards in the troubled-teen industry, and no federal standards of any kind. I was informed that legislation cannot address this lack of efficacy because private programs are not required to be proven safe or effective. Parents have the right to "put their kids wherever they want".

I believe that any law intended to prevent abuse within this industry should really begin with public awareness. One of the best ways to learn about the dynamics of abusive treatment programs is to read about Phillip Zimbardo's Lucifer Effect and the Stanford Prison Experiment. "Absolute power corrupts absolutely" and many programs are based on subjecting powerless kids to an absolutely powerful social system. This is a recipe for disaster, and it happens to be the very basis of many programs within the troubled-teen industry.

There is no safe way to restructure a teenager's psychology through aversive treatments and Pavlovian reconditioning methods.

Hopefully, federal legislation will also focus on psychological abuse, and will be based on a deep understanding of Robert J. Lifton's *Eight Criteria for Thought-Reform*. Each individual criteria for thought-reform ought to be prohibited from being used as a coercive measure. Detailed examples should be included that show how these methods have been used in programs throughout the last 50 years.

Coercive environments rely on built-in power imbalances that are a fertile breeding ground for sexual abuse, psychological torture, violent treatments and medical harm. But these are only symptoms of an underlying system of thought-reform. Addressing the symptoms could be a good first step if the root causes are also identified, understood and addressed.

There Is a System Behind the Abuse

The chronic abuses taking place in teen programs are nourished by the toxic combination of two poisons, a harmful *process* enabled by an extreme *environment*. The "therapeutic milieu" is meant to facilitate the "un-freezing" of the psychological structure of a client. But this "break 'em down, and build 'em up" process consistently causes psychological harm and goes hand in hand with extreme forms of cruelty. History shows us that although these methods are powerful, they are dangerous. There is no safe way to restructure a teenager's psychology through aversive treatments and Pavlovian re-conditioning methods. Wherever human kindness and basic contact with the world can only be earned through compliance; when communication with family is forbidden and the identity is assaulted; when a child is not allowed privacy or autonomy over bodily functions; when complaints are met with punishment; when a child is denied compassion and yet prevented from leaving; where "un-freezing" is forcibly coerced . . . abuse is being used as a "therapeutic tool". This type of social system is a "Bad Barrel" that will consistently produce "Bad Apples." *Why do we assume this behavior-change technology can ever be practiced safely?*

New Laws Are Unlikely to Change a Corrupt Legacy

Can legislation addresses the corruption that has enabled abuse throughout this industry's history? The little bit of research I've done tells me that coercive programs have *always* resulted in abuse and have *always* relied on legal corruption and the blind eye of state acquiescence.

America already has laws against abuse, we have standards and requirements and procedures. They have all been routinely and systematically ignored.

The US Department of Justice, the Department of Health and Human Services, the National Institute of Mental Health and many other federal agencies have been in bed with the behavior-modification industry from the beginning. Turning to any federal office for protection might be naïve at best. Many survivors of federally developed programs such as Straight Inc., say that the fox should not be guarding the hen-

45

house. One example would be the LEAA (Law Enforcement Assistance Agency), known to have been one of the main sources of funding for "beneficial brainwashing" programs within the adult and juvenile prison industry. Congress investigated many LEAA programs in the early 1970's and cut their federal funding due to gross ethical violations. The LEAA helped establish Straight Inc. with two large grants AFTER congress outlawed federal spending on behavior-modification programs. The LEAA was defamed and eventually re-named, today it's called DOJP . . . Department of Justice Programs.

Creating a new federal office in the Department of Health and Human Services (same bedroom as the DOJ) . . . ("Granny What Big Teeth You Have!") the fox becomes a wolf . . . and to think of spending millions and millions of dollars to do this . . . *without spending anything on research?* US Citizens will be paying millions of dollars to try to make an inherently abusive treatment, safer. It's like creating a public agency to make sure that all rapists wear condoms.

America already has laws against abuse, we have standards and requirements and procedures. They have all been routinely and systematically ignored. We already have laws, what we don't have is enforcement and more importantly, we don't have an understanding of the harm being done. We don't really understand the harmful effects of these "treatments" and we don't really understand the social dynamics that turn even the best people into abusers. When it comes to talking about legislation, it is impossible to prevent abuse that isn't understood.

Raising public awareness about the methods of coercion is one of the most powerful methods of preventing abuse.

The type of coercive reform I am speaking of begins with an assault on the very fabric of a clients psychological framework. This process of thought-reform or coercive-persuasion, consistently produces psychiatric casualties . . . the process it- self is harmful. The same methods that seem so mysterious and sinister within cults and communist re-education centers, are the exact same methods being used in many of today's "therapeutic" programs. [Psychiatrist] Joost Meerloo called it "Rape of the Mind." Even survivors who have experienced these methods first hand may not realize that the methods they were subjected to have been implemented by totalitarian powers the world over for thousands of years.

If measures that are intended to prevent abuse, assume that abuse simply occurs because of the "bad apples" we could inadvertently legitimize the "bad barrel". If our approach is to find a safe way to carry out an inherently harmful and unethi- cal process, we merely train rapists to wear condoms and we fail to address the real issues.

Raising Public Awareness Is the Only Way to Stop the Abuse

Raising public awareness about the methods of coercion is one of the most powerful methods of preventing abuse. In ad- dition to relying on the power of the government, we need to empower the general public and the professional community with knowledge of cultic dynamics and the principles of thought-reform. Light is the best disinfectant and awareness is the best innoculant. Rather than spending millions of dollars trying to tame a monstrous industry, perhaps we could spend millions of dollars raising awareness and developing safe and effective ways to meet the needs of our teenagers rather than merely changing them.

7

Kids for Cash

Warren Richey

Warren Richey is a journalist who has been a contributer to the Christian Science Monitor *for more than twenty years.*

Two judges in Pennsylvania have been found guilty of receiving kickbacks from private jail owners in return for funneling kids to their facilities. An examination of the judges' rulings showed little regard for the type of crime committed, as they consistently issued the harshest sentence of incarceration. Their goal was not justice but to keep the private facilities full, thus allowing the owners to receive millions of dollars in public money. Shocking as their crimes may seem, the two judges appear to be reflecting the attitude of the society around them. Americans are firm believers that the country needs to be tough on crime. It is inevitable then that some in the justice system would find a way to profit from these beliefs.

A former juvenile court judge in Pennsylvania was sentenced to 28 years in prison on Thursday [August 2011] for his part in an alleged "kids for cash" scam considered one of the worst judicial scandals in US history.

Mark Ciavarella Jr., 61, a former judge in Luzerne County, was also ordered to pay $1.17 million in restitution.

Mr. Ciavarella was convicted in federal court in Scranton, Pa., in February on charges that he and a second judge, Michael Conahan, ran the local court system as a racketeering enterprise.

Warren Richey, "Kids for Cash' Judge Sentenced to 28 Years for Racketeering Scheme, *Christian Science Monitor*, August 11, 2011. Copyright © 2011 by the Christian Science Monitor. All rights reserved. Reproduced by permission.

The federal indictment says the two judges accepted $2.8 million in kickbacks from the owner and builder of two privately-run juvenile detention facilities. In exchange, the judges agreed to close down the county's own juvenile detention center, which would have competed with the new, privately-run facilities. In addition they guaranteed that juvenile offenders from their court would be directed to the privately-run facilities.

Mr. Conahan, pleaded guilty last year to a single count of racketeering and is awaiting sentencing.

In comments to the court, Ciavarella apologized to the community and to the children whose cases he had adjudicated. "I blame no one but myself for what happened," he said, according to the Associated Press.

But the former judge rejected claims that he engaged in a "kids for cash" racketeering scheme. He said prosecutors used the claim to sabotage his reputation prior to his trial. "Those three words made me the personification of evil," he told the court, according to the Associated Press. "They made me toxic and caused a public uproar the likes of which this community has never seen."

The centers stood to profit from the higher number of juveniles they were housing.

Ciavarella had a reputation as a no-nonsense jurist who would not hesitate to sentence young, first-time offenders to juvenile detention. He also gained a reputation as a judge prone to cut constitutional corners.

An investigation revealed that half of the children who appeared in his courtroom were not represented by a lawyer and were never advised of their right to counsel. Of those unrepresented children, up to 60 percent were ordered by Ciavarella to serve time at a detention facility.

What was not known, prior to the federal investigation, was that Ciavarella and Conahan were receiving secret payments from the private detention centers. The centers stood to profit from the higher number of juveniles they were housing.

Amid mounting questions about Ciavarella's actions as a juvenile judge, the Pennsylvania Supreme Court in 2009 directed that all adjudications involving children appearing before Ciavarella from 2003 to 2008 be vacated and their records expunged. The directive is estimated to involve 4,000 cases.

One of those cases involved 16-year-old A.A., who was arrested for gesturing with her middle finger at a police officer who had been called during a custody dispute involving her parents and her sister.

According to a 2010 report of the Interbranch Pennsylvania Commission on Juvenile Justice, A.A. was an honor roll student, a Girl Scout, and YMCA member, who attended bible school. She had no prior arrest record and had never even been in detention in school.

She was sent to Ciavarella's court, and was told she wouldn't need a lawyer since it was a minor issue.

After examining the paperwork, Ciavarella informed A.A. that she had no respect for authority. She later told the investigating commission that Ciavarella never gave her an opportunity to speak at the hearing. She was led out of the courtroom in shackles and held in juvenile detention for six months.

After her release, A.A. returned to school and, again, qualified for the honor roll. She is currently in college and plans to pursue a law degree. She told the investigating commission that she wants to defend the legal rights of children.

Ciavarella was convicted of 12 of 39 counts in his indictment. The jury found him guilty of engaging in a pattern of racketeering and participating in a racketeering conspiracy through his receipt and transfer of $997,600 from individuals associated with the juvenile detention centers.

He was also convicted of failing to record the secret payments on judicial financial disclosure forms from 2004 to 2007, and for filing false tax returns for those same years. In addition, the jury found him guilty of engaging in a money-laundering conspiracy to conceal the payments

Prosecutors requested a life sentence.

Ciavarella says there was never a quid pro quo of providing juvenile offenders in exchange for money

---

In his sentencing memorandum, Ciavarella's lawyer, Albert Flora, urged US District Judge Edwin Kosik to issue a sentence on the lower end of the guidelines range.

"If Mark Ciavarella never did one day of incarceration, he would still be punished," Mr. Flora wrote. He said the former judge had been subject to "embarrassment, ridicule, and shame out of proportion to the offense."

"The media attention to this matter has exceeded coverage given to many and almost all capital murders, and despite protestations, he will forever be unjustly branded as the 'Kids for Cash' judge," Flora wrote.

Ciavarella has insisted that the money he received was not a bribe. He said it was a finder's fee legally paid to him for introducing the owner of the detention center business to a builder who was later awarded the contract to build the juvenile centers. Ciavarella says there was never a quid pro quo of providing juvenile offenders in exchange for money.

Judge Kosik rejected this reasoning while calculating Ciavarella's sentence.

"Defendant argues that the government planted a seed of the kids for cash idea without proof that the defendant sent kids away for cash," Kosik said in a pre-sentence ruling. "While there was no evidence of the number of kids put away, there was evidence of the defendant's financial interest [in the construction and operation of the juvenile detention centers]," the judge wrote.

At trial, a co-owner of the juvenile detention business, Robert Powell, testified that Ciavarella kept a record of the number of children he sent to the facility, as well as the amount of money the owners were making. According to court documents, Ciavarella allegedly told Mr. Powell: ". . . so it's not about me sending kids anymore. I know how much money you're making, and it's time to step up."

8

Criminal Justice Systems Now Favor Treatment Facilities Over Boot Camps

Will Di Novi

Will Di Novi is a former Nation *intern and currently a freelance journalist based in New York City.*

The juvenile justice system in the United States, which houses nearly eighty thousand people under the age of eighteen in detention and residential facilities across the nation, is and has been in a state of crisis for years, asserts Will Di Novi in the following viewpoint. However, the Senate is currently in the process of reauthorizing the Juvenile Justice and Delinquency Prevention Act of 1974, and Di Novi is confident the juvenile justice system in the United States may finally see some real change. The new iteration of the Act is designed to help keep children out of the juvenile system, where abuse has been endemic, instead favoring treatment facilities. On the local level, juvenile justice programs have been moving in this direction for the past decade, and it is high time for the federal government to follow suit, Di Novi concludes.

The girls at the Mississippi detention center were tied up for weeks at a time. Minor offenders, some as young as 13, were cuffed and chained when they ate or used the bathroom. In the words of Erica, a 16-year-old detainee, it was a place that "made you feel like you were nothing."

The boy was beaten and restrained by guards on his first day at a juvenile boot camp in Northwest Florida, suspected of faking an illness to avoid exercise. Martin Lee Anderson died from his injuries early the next day. He was 14.

David Burgos spent much of his young life running away from abusive group homes. One of the estimated 80 percent of juvenile offenders who suffer from a recognizable mental health disorder, the bipolar 17-year-old was arrested in 2006 for a probation violation related to a minor theft charge. After four months at Connecticut's Manson Youth Institution without mental health care, David hung himself with a bed sheet.

Poor Juvenile Delinquency Policies Increase Recidivism

According to the most recent data from the Office of Juvenile Justice and Delinquency Prevention, nearly 80,000 people under the age of 18 are held in juvenile detention and residential facilities around the United States each day. To juvenile justice advocates across the nation, the stories above are all too common in a system where punitive policies increase recidivism and exacerbate juvenile crime.

> *The Senate bill would also require the states to work towards reducing racial and ethnic disparities in the juvenile justice system.*

"We have a huge blind spot as a nation, an inability to see the human rights violations that are occurring here on our soil in our juvenile justice system," says Zachary Norris, Director of the Books Not Bars campaign at Oakland's Ella Baker Center, an initiative to reform California's youth prison system. "We often talk about how the [Iraq] war is expensive, but there's also our war on young people here in the United States that's incredibly wasteful."

Norris and other juvenile justice advocates now have their eyes turned to Congress, where ongoing legislative developments could produce the first meaningful response to this crisis in years. The Senate is currently in the process of reauthorizing the Juvenile Justice and Delinquency Prevention Act [JJDPA] of 1974, the federal legislation that sets standards for juvenile corrections systems in the states.

In addition to increasing federal funding for drug treatment, mental health care, and mentoring programs designed to keep children out of the juvenile system, the new iteration of the Act, Senate Bill 3155, includes an amendment to eliminate the incarceration of status offenders within three years of the bill's enactment. Status offenses are charges like truancy, running away or other offenses that would not be criminal if committed by an adult, and result in the incarceration of thousands of young people in some states, says the Washington, DC-based Coalition for Juvenile Justice.

The Senate bill would also require the states to work towards reducing racial and ethnic disparities in the juvenile justice system. Youth of color make up 34 percent of the American population below the age of eighteen but 62 percent of youth in juvenile detention, according to a report released last year by the National Council on Crime and Delinquency.

A Major Step Forward

While it's important to keep in mind the many abuses that the bill will not address—laws in more than forty states permitting adult courts to try children as young as 14, the sentencing of young offenders to terms of life without parole, the increasing criminalization of trivial misbehavior in schools—passage of the new iteration of the act would nonetheless represent a major step forward.

It would also recapture the spirit of progressive reform that propelled the JJDPA's initial passage over thirty years ago.

Under the original JJDPA of 1974, the states agreed to humanize their often Dickensian juvenile corrections systems in return for increased federal aid. This promising arrangement collapsed in the 1990s during what the *New York Times* has described as "hysteria about an adolescent crime wave that never materialized." Even as youth crime figures plummeted across the nation, stories of juvenile delinquency increased in the media and states intensified all kinds of punishments for children. Large numbers of juvenile offenders were sent to adult jails where, research has shown, they are more likely to be abused and transformed into repeat offenders. In Norris's estimation, "we are still seeing the repercussions of that movement" in the treatment of juvenile offenders today.

The new version of the JJDPA passed the Senate Judiciary Committee on July 31 with its major amendments intact and should soon advance to a full Senate vote. "Hundreds of organizations throughout the country, including some unlikely allies, have voiced strong support for the juvenile justice reforms in the Act," says Carol Chodroff, US Advocacy Director at Human Rights Watch. "There is significant recognition from a vast array of stakeholders in the juvenile justice system—including many law enforcement organizations—that we cannot arrest our way out of the problem of juvenile crime and delinquency."

A More Promising Approach

A far more promising approach has been playing out on the local level. Over the past decade, Missouri's juvenile corrections system has been celebrated for a rehabilitation-oriented model that invests in small community-based centers, keeps young offenders near their homes to participate in family therapy, and helps young people with job placement and therapy referrals upon their release. Missouri has achieved the lowest recidivism rate in the nation.

In Pima County, Arizona, where "scared straight" policies once produced such rampant incarceration that the local juvenile detention facility had young people sleeping in a cafeteria; a local partnership with the Anne E. Casey Foundation's Juvenile Detention Alternatives Initiative has drastically reduced the juvenile prison population. The number of children arrested for violent or property crimes dropped 43 percent between 1997 and 2006 and the county's presiding Juvenile Court Judge says there has been no increase in juvenile crime despite the lower incarceration rate.

"If you have youths wondering, 'Am I a good person or a bad person?' and you put those young people in detention, you're confirming this is who they are and this is who we expect them to be," Judge Patricia Escher told the *Arizona Daily Star* in June. "When you detain young people inappropriately, what you do is send them on a path of criminality."

In Zachary Norris's estimation, Congress must keep the success of these programs in mind as it assesses the new JJDPA. It is time, he says, to ask "What programs actually build on the strength of young people? Help them get job skills? There's a recognition that tough-on-crime policies hurt us. If kids are worse off when they return [from detention], then we're worse off as a whole."

"We've still got a row to hoe," says Tara Andrews, deputy executive director of the Coalition for Juvenile Justice, looking ahead with cautious optimism to the JJDPA's progress before Congress. "But when you start seeing all the work that's being done, you realize there's not isolated pockets of reform. You realize a platform for change is being built."

9

Therapeutic Teen Treatment Programs Lead to Less Recidivism

Gina Gaston

Gina Gaston is a television journalist and co-anchor at KTRK-ABC 13 in Houston, Texas.

A boot camp style approach has proven to be a less effective model for rehabilitating troubled youth. Increasingly, judges, courts, and families are turning to programs that emphasize therapy and a more individualized delivery. These programs can prove to be just as strict as the old boot camps but focus on individual problems rather than forcing teens to conform to group needs. Preliminary results show that more therapeutic methods reduce recidivism rates and enable youngsters to make the changes needed to be more successful.

When it comes to rehabilitating troubled kids, there is a new approach in Harris County [Texas]. The strict boot-camp style tactics are being replaced with more one-on-one therapy.

The young men have been in trouble with the law, and a judge hopes to stop the cycle. One 15-year-old pulled a knife on his own dad.

"We were arguing and I just grabbed it to tell him to back off and he just called the cops on me," the teen said.

But now there's been a change.

"I took classes with a counselor, she taught me how to relax," the teen said. "But right now, I don't get aggressive real fast, so I'm a pretty calm person now," the teen said.

This kind of counseling is the cornerstone of the curriculumn at the Harris County Leadership Academy; up early, in classes most of the day, and then group and one-on-one counseling.

"The approach is much more individualized than it used to be in years back so now we focus on what are the skills that you need, what are the issues, the risk factors that are going on in your life that are making you act in delinquent ways," said Diana Quintana with the Harris County Leadership Academy.

While instructors are still strict, barking at students has been replaced by talking and listening.

At one time, boot camps were the main form of rehabilitation for troubled kids. Instructors would break the child down and build them back up, much like they do in the military.

"Our research has shown that the boot-camp style program is not as effective in terms of curbing delinquent behavior," Quintana said.

Quintana says that's because the idea behind a boot camp is to teach them to work as a team. But in a place like this, teenagers are not here for teamwork, they have individual needs.

And while instructors are still strict, barking at students has been replaced by talking and listening.

"The Juvenile Justice System is about rehabilitation, it's about rehabilitating kids, so we focus on what skills that we need to give you to make you more successful and be a productive member of society, as to being out there committing delinquent crimes," Quintana said.

So is it working? According to preliminary numbers, yes.

The Number of Repeat Offenders Is Decreasing

Tom Brooks oversees the Harris County Juvenile Department and says since moving away from the boot camp style in 2010, there's been a decrease in repeat offenders.

"With the boot camp, the statistics show we had about a 25 percent recidivism rate; since we've moved to the therapeutic programs it's about a 20 percent and we are happy with that, that's very successful," Brooks said.

On this day, the teens were listening to an adult who served time for murder.

"I wonder what kind of change I could have made in myself if I would have had this opportunity," the speaker said.

He's hoping his story serves as a warning, a warning for teenagers like one 16-year old who is serving four months for violating parole. Soon he'll return home to the same neighborhood, same friends and same potential pitfalls.

"Are you nervous about being free again?" we asked the teen.

"Yes ma'am, I'm nervous," the teen said.

"What are you scared about?"

"To lose control and then get arrested and go back to the same life as before I got locked up."

This time, though, the teens will be armed with something different.

"They learned skills through the programs and these are things that they can use when they are back in the community that will continue, which goes a lot further than just the discipline they had with the previous program," Brooks said.

Special Therapy Programs Teach Teens to Care for Others

Project HEEL is one of the county's therapy programs, and it involves stray dogs. The kids and dogs are locked up behind walls, and to get out and make it in the real world, they will have to work together.

"The expectations for Corridor Rescue was to help make our dogs more adoptable," said Dawn Ruben with Project HEEL.

A teenager and a dog are teamed up for eight weeks.

"The dogs respond very well to the kids and it builds their self confidence; they learn a lot about the anatomy of the dog, they learn how to work with the dogs out in the community," Brooks said.

For both, it's a chance to start fresh.

"It's a beginning for the dog and it's a beginning for them too," Ruben said.

"I honestly can say it's a privilege to work with these animals, to be able to get a benefit from it, to take it back out into the free and do something positive with it," a 17-year-old in the program said.

They're skills and knowledge that were not always translating with the hard and harsh style of boot camp.

"It's really helping me. It's helping me become a better person," a 15-year-old said.

And then there's the gardening program, which teaches patience, nurturing, and most importantly, the ability to land a job.

"What the thought for them to do is get to actually get a job or try to receive a job in the horticulture industry," said Phillicia Moore, who runs the gardening program at the academy.

They're skills and knowledge that were not always translating with the hard and harsh style of boot camp. . . .

The cost of the therapy programs is minimal. Project HEEL is totally run by volunteers with no cost to the state. The gardening program has a budget of $30,000 a year, but again, those funds come from [an] outside source.

No matter what the cost, the rewards are proving priceless.

"It teaches you how to care for something else instead of being selfish all the time," the 15-year-old said.

"This is a great opportunity that I have right now. And I plan to take it out and turn my negative activity I was doing into something positive," the 17-year-old said.

10

The Tough Love Approach Used By Boot Camps Is Harmful and Abusive

William Norman Grigg

William Norman Grigg is the author of several books from a Constitutionalist perspective, and was formerly a senior editor for The New American.

Parents who feel they can no longer control their children sometimes turn to boot camps for help. However, abuse is systemic in the behavior modification (BM) industry, of which boot camps are only one example. There is little evidence that harsh, cruel treatment of juveniles endemic at these BM facilities may do any help. Often, the reality is that the treatment will not only fail to change the child for good but prove to be so traumatic that the child is worse off emotionally and behaviorally than before the camp.

Martin Lee Anderson was sent to a "boot camp" for delinquents in Bay County, Florida, on January 5 [2006] for violating the terms of his probation. The slender, rangy 14-year-old collapsed during the camp's introductory calisthenics program. Evacuated by helicopter to a Pensacola hospital, Anderson died the next day.

The Bay County coroner concluded that Anderson died from natural causes related to sickle cell trait. The young

William Norman Grigg, "'Tough love'—or Torture?" *The New American*, vol. 22, no. 6, March 20, 2006, p. 44. Copyright © 2006 by The New American. All rights reserved. Reproduced by permission.

man's family, and others who reviewed an hour and 20 minute videotape taken by security cameras, believe that Anderson died as the result of being beaten for a half hour by guards.

State representative Gustavo Barreiro, the Republican chair of the legislature's Criminal Justice Appropriations Committee, reports that the video depicted the unresisting teenager being repeatedly hit, kicked, and kneed by a swarm of large adult males. "When you see stuff like that," Rep. Barreiro observed, "you want to go through the TV and say, 'Enough is enough.'"

Many of them were forcibly taken from their beds early in the morning by rented thugs who—with parental authorization—seized the teens, restrained them with handcuffs if necessary, and delivered them into the custody of the BM programs.

Boot Camps and the Behavior Modification Industry

The episode offers a terrifying glimpse of the "behavior modification" (BM) industry, of which teen boot camps are merely one example.

BM programs are advertised as a variety of "tough love." This concept appeals to the reasonable belief that some adolescents inclined toward violent crime or self-destructive behavior need both strong discipline (toughness) and compassion (love). This approach, when built on a foundation of biblical principles, can and does yield positive results, since it is designed to cultivate within each participant a sense of responsibility—to others and to himself—within the framework of God's law.

BM programs, however, are secular exercises in tearing down willful personalities and re-casting them as conformists. Where the approach typified by Father Flanagan and his legendary "Boys Town" is motivated by Christian charity, the motives of many involved in the BM industry are mercenary and ideological.

The boot camp where Anderson died, notes the February 27 *Naples News*, was one of roughly 50 camps established in 30 states beginning in the late 1980s. Studies on recidivism rates of boot camp graduates, including a 2004 report from the National Institutes of Health, have documented "little if any improvement from more traditional juvenile justice programs."

In addition to boot camps, there is a network of quasi-private BM programs, some of which operate offshore in Mexico, Costa Rica, Jamaica, Samoa, and elsewhere. Others are wilderness programs like the one featured in the short-lived ABC "reality" series Brat Camp. Tens of thousands of American teenagers are enrolled in such programs. Many of them were forcibly taken from their beds early in the morning by rented thugs who—with parental authorization—seized the teens, restrained them with handcuffs if necessary, and delivered them into the custody of the BM programs.

Systematic Sadism

Most of the abductees are not criminals, but merely the rebellious offspring of parents who have been convinced by the BM industry that ordinary adolescent misbehavior is symptomatic of potentially lethal problems. Those problems, of course, can only be solved—for the price of an Ivy League education—through BM programs, which though advertised as "tough love," too often amount to little more than systematic sadism.

Many BM programs, writes Maia Szalavitz in her new book *Help at Any Cost*, "utilize punishments banned for use on criminals and by the Geneva Conventions. Beatings, extended isolation and restraint, public humiliation, food deprivation, sleep deprivation, forced exercise to the point of exhaustion, sensory deprivation, and lengthy maintenance of stress positions are common."

At one BM facility in Puerto Rico, writes Szalavitz, "teens were found bound and gagged with nooses around their necks." In 2001, Mexican authorities discovered a facility run by the Utah-based World Wide Association of Specialty Programs [and Schools] (WWASPS) in which teens had been locked in dog cages. At a WWASPS camp in Samoa, refractory teens were sentenced to lengthy confinement in a three-foot by three-foot box similar to North Vietnamese "tiger cages."

Amberly Knight, a WWASPS whistle-blower who administered a camp in Costa Rica, testified that American "children were imprisoned in deplorable conditions that we would not tolerate for adult death row inmates in America." When the atrocities at Abu Ghraib [prison in Iraq] were made public, Knight was "horrified," because "that's what they do [at some WWASPS facilities] every single day."

The pedigree of contemporary BM programs can be traced to a now-defunct federally funded program called The Seed.

A Communist-Derived Approach

A 1974 investigation by the Senate Judiciary Committee found that The Seed employed methods similar to the "highly refined 'brainwashing' techniques employed by the North Koreans" against U.S. prisoners of war.

While honorable people can disagree about the best way to deal with troubled teens, there's little reason to doubt that the communist-derived BM approach is the worst.

11

MTV's Portrayal of Teen Treatment Centers Is Misleading

Shain Neumeier

Shain Neumeier is a law clerk for the Community Alliance for the Ethical Treatment of Youth (CAFETY) and a law student at Suffolk University Law School in Boston, Massachusetts.

The producers of the MTV series True Life *have done a disservice to its teen audience in an episode dealing with two teens who have been sent to private residential treatment centers. The show presents a slanted portrayal of how each of the two teens and their families faced a particularly difficult time. The teens are assumed to be guilty of any accusations made against them and the choice of being sent away seems to be the first and only option for the families. Any other possibilities, such as therapy or a treatment program that is local, are never considered until after the boot camp experience. This show reinforced damaging beliefs about youth and institution-based treatment.*

Even if a person knows little to nothing about the private youth residential treatment industry, the title of MTV's *True Life*'s latest episode, "I'm Being Sent Away by My Parents," may very well evoke some strong emotions—fear, sadness, anger, abandonment or even betrayal, to name a few possibilities. This title would suggest that the episode would address and take seriously the concerns, feelings and experiences of youth who are sent far from their homes to attend private wilderness programs, therapeutic boarding schools, boot camps and other residential programs for "troubled" or "struggling" teens. Instead, the fears of youth rights advocates surrounding this portrayal of two such programs that would effectively stand in for an entire industry with a long history of abuse and fraudulent treatment practices were confirmed as soon as the introductory voiceover began.

True Life, which might be best described as a combination between a reality show and a series of documentaries on young adult life, has a consistent format—a legitimate stylistic choice, but one that by itself limits the amount and kind of information that an episode can provide on its subject matter. Each episode follows two teenagers or young adults in dealing with the issue presented in the episode's title, whether it be "I Have an Embarrassing Medical Condition," "I Have a Fetish," or, in this case, "I'm Being Sent Away by My Parents." It opens with a brief introduction which includes clips from later in the episode and a voiceover summarizing the issue as it affects the two young people that the episode focuses on. From then on, though, there are no more voiceovers or other explicit commentary by the makers of the show themselves, and the show switches to telling the "story" by following the people it features around with a camera and interviewing various people that it introduces throughout the episode. The end of the episode will show how the two young people have resolved the central issue or closely related ones, for better or worse.

Objectivity Lost from the Beginning of the Show

In spite of this at least superficially hands-off approach, the makers of *True Life* made their support of the use of wilderness programs, therapeutic boarding schools and other residential programs as a means of addressing rebellious teenage behavior very clear, not only through the episode's introduction but through editing and "storytelling" choices made throughout the rest of it. As mentioned earlier, the show's voiceover sets the tone for the rest of the episode. "What if you were causing so much trouble for your parents that they sent you to live far away from home as a last resort to improve your troubling behavior?" it starts by asking the audience. It ends with another question: "Will [the two teens featured in the episode] learn to tow the line, or keep wreaking havoc?" The outright bias against these teenagers, their perspectives and their behavior is further demonstrated by how the end of each commercial break is marked by someone saying, "You're going to bad boy camp."

A lot of what is shown, and how it was shown, actually was problematic or carried unfortunate implications.

The episode follows Kyle, who is 14 years old and whose mother has sent him to a Christian "no-nonsense boarding school" called Jubilee, and Spencer, a 16 year old sent by his mother to the Anasazi Foundation wilderness program. Kyle is made to attend Jubilee because he has been engaging in drug use, theft and other criminal activity. Meanwhile, Spencer's family sends him to Anasazi because his grief over the recent death of his father has caused him to become sullen and apathetic. The show does not address whether and to what extent either boy has received mental health treatment or other services and supports in their communities before being sent off to their respective residential programs.

Quality of Treatment Programs Left Unexplored

The show, in fact, does not cover a large number of things, which made it very hard to accurately judge the quality of the programs. Some of this can be attributed to the medium and the format of the show, in that the episode has slightly less than 50 minutes to tell two stories that occur over a period of weeks or months. However, even within these constraints, there were questions that the show could have and should have answered. For instance, what kind of therapy or drug rehabilitation was Kyle receiving at Jubilee? How were the wilderness and survival aspects of the Anasazi program used to address Spencer's grief and resulting difficulties? What kind of educational opportunities did either boy have access to in their respective programs? What, even, was the day-to-day routine at these programs? Without knowing the answers to these and other questions, it was hard to tell if either or both of these programs were one of those schools—the kind which routinely abuse and neglect the children in their care in the name of behavior modification or even therapy—or one of the exemplary and truly therapeutic residential programs that many parents and a fair number of program alumni say exist.

A lot of what is shown, and how it was shown, actually was problematic or carried unfortunate implications. For instance, from what is shown on screen, the extent of Spencer's rebellious, unmanageable behavior seems to be that he was easily annoyed with his mother, unmotivated when it comes to school, and unwilling to play with his little brother. These are normal, or at least common, teenage behaviors even for people who are not reeling from the recent death of a beloved parent. The show does not, and really cannot, effectively make these out to be behaviors requiring a "last resort" approach. On the other hand, the show does not in any way elaborate on a scene where Spencer tells his friend that this world is "not a good place to live in anymore"—language that quite clearly indicates depression or something like it—in favor of focusing on how his "confrontational attitude" is hurting the adults around him. This is reflected in the scene where Spencer reunites with his mother at the end of his time in the Anasazi Foundation program. Spencer's counselor, in talking with them both, asks Spencer whether he has anything to say to his mother regarding how he was acting before he attended the program, and in response to this, Spencer apologizes to her for what he said to her before he left. While the fact that he made amends for the things he feels he should is all well and good, this was noticeably one-sided, at least on screen. This leaves the audience to wonder whether it was the counselor, the filmmakers or both who did not think that the mother should have at least been asked the same question.

> *There is no way for a viewer to know whether the program's expectations and practices are really as reasonable as the show implies, or if editing . . . has considerably softened them.*

A Problematic Approach to Discipline

It is obvious from the beginning that Kyle's behavioral problems, unlike Spencer's, go well beyond normal teenage surliness. Still, the show itself makes it clear through Kyle's introduction that he is a product of a broken home—complete with an abusive father, an unpleasant divorce and a brother who also engages in drug use and criminal activity—rather than its cause. There is even footage to imply that some of his problems may result from serious self-esteem issues, with Kyle speculating with resignation in his voice that his mother is "happy . . . [she's] gonna get rid of this little shit bag who's stealing [her] jewelry" when he is accepted into Jubilee. The audience is left to wonder why a Christian boarding school would more effectively address these various issues than would a therapist, a support group or any number of other community resources, or whether Kyle's mother even considered these options before enrolling him at Jubilee, as the show does not ask or answer these questions.

To someone who is familiar with the practices of abusive residential programs for youth, Jubilee's program raises several red flags just by what is shown in the episode. It makes use of a level system, giving students whose behavior it approves of special status that comes with enhanced privileges (such as larger rooms) and supervisory authority over other, lower-level students. Also, as the show acknowledges and another student tells the audience in an explanation riddled with program-speak, the punishments for misbehavior can be serious. If you get a "write-up," you can be given "consequences," which include "running five hills" (being made to run up and down a steep hill next to the school five times), or, if you fail to run your hills and the extra hills added on as consequences, you can be placed on "room restriction" or "meal restriction." Finally, Kyle's phone calls with his mother—which he is only allowed to make after some indeterminate length of time spent at the program—are monitored by a staff member who is sitting in the room listening to the call on speakerphone. The way in and extent to which Jubilee makes use of the aforementioned practices is unclear, but in light of how all of them—level systems, strenuous exercise as punishment, food-based punishments, seclusion and restricted access to one's family—have been used by various residential programs to horrifically abusive effect, they provide legitimate cause for suspicion and concern on the part of youth, families and viewers alike. Statements by the staff that Kyle's refusing to run hills or otherwise do as he is told is just making things harder on himself, as well as a warning by an upper-level student during a pre-admission tour that Kyle's stay at Jubilee would go very slowly if he tried to fight the program, did nothing to alleviate this sense of unease.

Teen's Criticism of Treatment Is Ignored

Despite these warning signs, the show portrays Kyle's belief that Jubilee is "like a jail for kids" as unfounded, and his resistance to its program as wrongheaded. On at least two separate occasions, the show cuts directly between sound or video clips in which Kyle talks about how much he dislikes the program and ones in which he acts out and then complains when he gets punished, inviting the audience to dismiss his complaints as unjustified or exaggerated because of his behavior. Because of this, there is no way for a viewer to know whether the program's expectations and practices are really as reasonable as the show implies, or if editing (or for that matter, the presence of the camera) has considerably softened them.

True Life's "I'm Being Sent Away by My Parents" could have given a voice to the concerns and experiences of youth sent to residential programs . . . [but] instead reinforced ideas about . . . institution-based care that are already far too widely held.

Perhaps the most troubling aspect of the episode was the ending, and all the implications it carried. Spencer, who, according to the show, came to the conclusion to give the wilderness program a chance and work towards starting a new life after one hour of meditation near the top of a mountain, reunites with his family at the end of the wilderness program, and goes on to attend family therapy with his mother after returning home (the show provided no explanation as to why no one thought to try family or other therapy before using the "last resort" of residential treatment). Kyle, on the other hand, continued to dislike and resist the program at Jubilee, and actively tried to get expelled. When he finally succeeded in getting sent home, he was shown to have been convicted of malicious mischief for vandalism and charged with possession of drug paraphernalia and assault soon after, and eventually sent to a boy's ranch similar to Jubilee. While all of this is true, the way in which it was presented suggested that Spencer's completion of the wilderness program and Kyle's expulsion from the boarding school were the sole causes of their respective outcomes. This conclusion is just not supported by the other information presented in the episode, where the types and severity of the two boys' problems were so different, where Spencer had apparently grown up with a more stable home life than had Kyle, and where there is no indication that Kyle received any sort of counseling or support in the community after returning home, family or otherwise.

True Life Fails to Present the Flip Side of "Tough Love"

Furthermore, the assumption underlying this message, namely that the measure of whether residential programs are appropriate for youth is how successful they are in curbing aberrant or just simply annoying teenage behavior, is similarly flawed. It ignores the negative and often traumatizing effects that a treatment philosophy based on "tough love," and for that matter residential treatment itself, can have on youth. In fact, it ignores the interests of youth almost entirely, placing their interests in freedom, security, continued inclusion in their communities, and even effective treatment second to adult expectations regarding everything from their conduct down to their demeanor. The existence of the most extreme residential behavioral modification programs for youth serves as proof of exactly how dangerous this assumption can be when allowed to go as unexamined as it was in this episode.

One can't expect a show like *True Life*, with its reality TV-style format and its focus on individual stories and circumstances, to provide an in-depth, comprehensive exposé of the so-called "troubled teen industry" and its practices. However, that doesn't excuse it from all responsibility in how it frames and then addresses the issues surrounding residential treatment for youth. In the end, the creators of the show chose to portray Spencer's grief over his father's death as rebellious and disrespectful behavior. They chose to edit the clips of Kyle's stay at Jubilee in such a way as to undermine the largely unspecified but quite possibly legitimate complaints he had about the program. They chose to skim over aspects of the programs that raised red flags. Finally, they chose to end the episode on the note that these programs, and the behavioral changes that ostensibly result from participating in them, make all the difference between extremely positive and extremely negative outcomes for youth with family, mental health and behavioral issues. *True Life*'s "I'm Being Sent Away by My Parents" could have given a voice to the concerns and experiences of youth sent to residential programs, whose own voices at this point have largely gone unheard or been dismissed. It could have even given a (truly) balanced portrayal of the perspectives of parents, program staff and youth. In part because of these missed opportunities, it is disappointing that the show instead reinforced ideas about teenagers, discipline and institution-based care that are already far too widely held, go far too unexamined and, as a result, are far too damaging to many youth who could have benefited from less punishment and more effective support than is provided at "last resort" residential programs.

12

Weight Loss Camps Teach Kids to Make Healthy Choices

PRWeb

PRWeb is the leader in online news distribution and online publicity.

The following viewpoint highlights the opening of a new camp for Camp Shane, the longest running fitness and weight loss camp for kids. Camp Shane, a premier youth weight loss camp, is a good example of successful weight loss camps that focus on healthy choices to change the habits of campers who struggle with obesity. Diverse activities, such as sports, water activities, nutrition, and cooking classes balance fun with fitness, and teach children lifelong skills.

Camp Shane, the longest running fitness and weight loss camp for kids, has opened a new camp in Georgia, three miles from the North Carolina border. Parents in the Southeast with overweight children wanting to experience the healthy lifestyle benefits of Camp Shane, now have the option of a location closer to home.

Camp Shane's newest summer camp, encompasses more than 1,200 acres of picturesque landscape and has an on-site lake, indoor pool, and professional grade sport and fitness facilities. The program offers weight loss camps in two, four or six week increments.

Weight Loss Camps Empower Children

Through an overriding commitment to care, parents have entrusted Camp Shane to fight childhood obesity since 1968. By providing fun and educational activities about healthy living choices, Camp Shane empowers children with the knowledge they need to completely re-shape their lives.

Camp Shane also offers an array of cooking and nutritional classes to help children learn the importance of portion control.

Through an easy, yet effective nutrition program, focusing on everyday foods and portion control, as well as exciting outdoor activities, the children at Camp Shane can expect to not only lose weight and learn how to keep it off, but also have fun, learn new skills and gain the confidence they deserve. In addition to children's weight loss camps, Camp Shane offers a weight loss programs for Young Adults 18 to 25 and a weight loss resort program for adults 18 and over.

"At Camp Shane, we're not a 'fat camp, diet or boot camp.' Instead of focusing solely on dieting, Camp Shane is an exciting and educational program that helps teach children realistic and achievable ways to maintain a healthy lifestyle. Every child at Camp Shane is treated as part of our family, and our dedication has helped us become the most recognized children's weight loss camp in the country," says David Ettenberg, Owner/Director of Camp Shane.

Diverse activities available at Camp Shane include sports, fitness, arts and crafts and exciting pool recreational activities. Camp Shane also offers an array of cooking and nutritional classes to help children learn the importance of portion control, as well as how to make healthy selections when dining out.

Teens Seeking Camps Have Many Choices

Although it is a premier youth weight loss camp, Camp Shane maintains competitive mid-range pricing to ensure its services are available to all children who need to lose weight.

"Camp Shane is a camp that everyone is proud to be a part of—staff, parents and kids. It gives us such joy to see the difference that Camp Shane can make in a child's life," says Ettenberg.

Camp Shane, since 1968, the premier youth fitness and weight loss camp facility, has been dedicated to fighting obesity in children and teens. Camp Shane offers camp locations in New York, California and now Georgia, featuring healthy menus, nutrition education, self-esteem building and traditional fun activities. By empowering children with the knowledge and skills they need to make healthy living choices, Camp Shane has helped countless children re-shape their lives and gain the self-confidence they deserve.

Shane Diet & Fitness Resorts for adults offers a summer program from one to twelve weeks, and is scheduled to open a year-round program in spring of 2012.

Shane Cares, a non-profit weight loss camp for underprivileged children, is scheduled to open in summer of 2012.

13

Solid Data Is Lacking to Support Residential Treatment of Eating Disorders

John M. Grohol

John M. Grohol is a doctor of psychology and the editor-in-chief and founder of Psych Central, a website that provides mental health information and advocacy for more than two million visitors each month.

There is a surprising lack of solid research to support the use of residential treatment centers for eating disorders. While many experts defend this expensive treatment method, they cannot produce the evidence to back up their opinion, because relatively few studies have been conducted. The treatment of eating disorders is complex and often involves many failed attempts before lasting change occurs. The industry is doing itself a disservice in not investing in a well-designed, scientific study that closely examines program effectiveness.

There's a lucrative cottage industry in the U.S. for the residential treatment of almost anything you can imagine. Everything from "Internet addiction" and drug and alcohol problems, to eating and mood disorders. If you can treat it in an outpatient setting, the thinking goes, why not treat it in a "residential" setting for 30 or more days where you control every aspect of the patient's life?

The "residential" treatment approach has long been available for eating disorders, since the treatment of these disorders tends to be long and complicated. Andrew Pollack writing for the *New York Times* notes how these kinds of programs have now become the focus of insurance companies looking to cut back on treatment options.

It's no surprise, really. With the rollout of mental health parity—requiring that insurance companies can no longer discriminate against people with mental disorders for their treatment options—those companies are looking for other places they can cut costs. Residential treatment for eating disorders appears to be one obvious area.

So is residential treatment a legitimate modality for helping people with eating disorders? Should insurance companies cover the costs of such care?

According to one study . . . , the average length of stay in a residential treatment center for an eating disorder is 83 days. That's nearly 3 months of full-time, round-the-clock treatment and care. The cost for such care? On average, it's $956 per day. You read that right—nearly $1,000/day is the average cost for such care. That means a single patient at such a treatment center is bringing in, on average, $79,348.

There is some research data in the literature. But surprisingly very little, and nothing approaching a randomized controlled study—the gold standard of research.

Available Data Does Little to Support Residential Treatment

Proponents of residential treatment admit there's little research to back its use for eating disorders, but are adamant such programs are effective and needed:

> Dr Anne E. Becker, president of the Academy of Eating Disorders and director of the eating disorders program at Mas-

sachusetts General Hospital, said that despite a paucity of studies, "There's no question that residential treatment is life-saving for some patients."

Okay. But so is spiritual healing, according to many spiritual healers. What separates belief (the mainstay of religion) from fact (the mainstay of science) is data. Without data, we operate in a vacuum of knowledge.

Ah, but we apparently do have *some* data. Just not the kind that a residential treatment center wants to hear:

> Ira Burnim, legal director of the Bazelon Center for Mental Health Law, which litigates for better mental health treatments, said that while he was not familiar with eating disorders, "study after study" had shown that residential centers for other mental or emotional disorders were not as effective as treatment at home.[. . .]

> "There's a wide variation in licensing across the country," said Jena L. Estes, vice president for the federal employee program at the Blue Cross and Blue Shield Association. "There's a lack of oversight of many of those residential treatment centers."

There is *some* research data in the literature. But surprisingly very little, and nothing approaching a randomized controlled study—the gold standard of research. For instance, in Bean et al. (2004), the researchers did a 15-month phone followup with folks who had anorexia who had stayed at their residential treatment center. According to this study, women experienced a 7 lb weight gain, while men experienced an average of a 19 lb weight gain.

But we have no idea whether these are good or bad numbers. Would someone in outpatient treatment over the same time period experience more or less weight gain? Are these numbers even accurate, given they are self-reported by the patient over the telephone (and the research was conducted by biased researchers at their own treatment center)? So we have "data" here, but without context, it's next to meaningless.

Another study by Bean & Weltzin (2001) showed that after a 6 month followup, anorexic and bulimic women retained some, but not all, of the improvements they made while in treatment. Again, without an outpatient or control group, it's hard to say whether this is a good or bad finding.

Eating disorders are unique, and perhaps even more unique than drug and alcohol problems—therefore deserving of special treatment.

There's also a few dissertations that offer similar evidence—when pre- versus post-measures are used in a residential treatment program, most patients are improved at discharge. This is hardly a surprising finding. But is it due to the "treatment" portion of the program, or the "residential" component—or some important combination thereof—remains unanswered.

Insurance Companies Challenge Validity of Treatment with Good Reason

So I hate to say it, but the insurance companies in this case appear to have a pretty good case, at least based upon the paucity of research. I always say to people, if you want to shut up an insurance company, show them the research that your treatment modality works (and works better than cheaper treatment X).

For better or worse, judges don't have to care about the research, and in this case ruled against the insurance company where the issue of paying for residential treatment for an eating disorder was brought to court:

The Ninth Circuit Appeals judges, based in San Francisco, ruled that residential treatment was medically necessary for eating disorders, and therefore had to be covered under the state's parity law, even if no exact equivalent existed on the physical disease side.

Eating disorders *are* unique, and perhaps even more unique than drug and alcohol problems—therefore deserving of special treatment. After all, unlike alcohol or drugs, we all have to eat. The way eating disorders wrap themselves up into the person's mind and their body image is very difficult to untangle.

But if we want people to have access to residential treatment centers to help with their eating disorders, shouldn't the industry support far more well-designed, scientific studies to examine the effectiveness of this modality? I don't think anybody would question these centers if such research existed today, but the fact that it doesn't after more than 25 years raises more than just a few eyebrows.

Organizations to Contact

The editors have compiled the following list of organizations concerned with the issues debated in this book. The descriptions are derived from materials provided by the organizations. All have publications or information available for interested readers. The list was compiled on the date of publication of the present volume; names, addresses, phone and fax numbers, and e-mail and Internet addresses may change. Be aware that many organizations take several weeks or longer to respond to inquiries, so allow as much time as possible.

Alliance for the Safe, Therapeutic and Appropriate Use of Residential Treatment (ASTART)
c/o Dr. Robert Friedman, University of South Florida
Department of Child and Family Studies
13301 Bruce B. Downs Blvd., Tampa, FL   33612
website: www.astartforteens.org

The Alliance for the Safe, Therapeutic and Appropriate Use of Residential Treatment is a community of professionals, family members, and survivors working to protect children from abuse and neglect in residential programs, and ensure families have safe and effective community-based care. The alliance attempts to refute the common reasons many families consider residential programs with practical advice and research-based material.

Annie E. Casey Foundation
701 St. Paul St., Baltimore, MD   21202
(410) 547-6600 • fax: (410) 547-6624
e-mail: webmail@aecf.org
website: www.aecf.org

The Annie E. Casey Foundation is a private charitable organization dedicated to helping build better futures for disadvantaged children in the United States. The primary mission of the foundation is to foster public policies, human service reforms, and community supports that more effectively meet the needs of today's vulnerable children and families. Its publications include "The Missouri Model," which explores alternatives to current treatment facilities with a focus on improving outcomes for incarcerated youth.

Coalition for Juvenile Justice (CJJ)

1319 F St. NW, Suite 402, Washington, DC   20004
(202) 467-0864 • fax: (202) 887-0738
e-mail: info@juvjustice.org
website: www.juvjustice.org

CJJ is a nationwide coalition of State Advisory Groups (SAGs) and allies dedicated to preventing children and youth from becoming involved in the courts and upholding the highest standards of care when youth are charged with wrongdoing and enter the justice system. Details about CJJ's "SOS" Project—Safety, Opportunity & Success: "Standards of Care for Non-Delinquent Youth" can be found on its website.

Community Alliance for the Ethical Treatment of Youth (CAFETY)

PO Box 1319, New York, NY   10163
(877) 322-3389
e-mail: admin@cafety.org
website: www.cafety.org

CAFETY is a member-driven advocacy organization that promotes and secures the human rights of youth in or at risk of residential placement. CAFETY believes every child, including children exhibiting emotional and behavioral differences, have the right to live with family and be included in their community. Its "Care, NOT Coercion Campaign" works to increase awareness of states that house residential programs that are coercive and operate under a philosophy or use practices that undermine the dignity of youth.

Justice Policy Institute

1012 14th St. NW, Suite 400, Washington, DC   20005
(202) 558-7974
e-mail: info@justicepolicy.org
website: www.justicepolicy.org

Justice Policy Institute is a national nonprofit organization that advances policies that promote well-being and justice for all people and communities. The institute envisions a society with safe, equitable, and healthy communities; just and effective solutions to social problems; and alternatives to incarceration that promote positive life outcomes. Recent briefs examine the intersection of youth employment and public safety in Washington, DC, and explore proactive approaches to reducing youth involvement in treatment and correctional facilities.

National Eating Disorders Association (NEDA)

165 W 46th St., New York, NY   10036
(212) 575-6200
e-mail: info@NationalEatingDisorders.org
website: www.nationaleatingdisorders.org

The National Eating Disorders Association is a nonprofit organization dedicated to supporting individuals and families affected by eating disorders. NEDA campaigns for prevention, improved access to quality treatment, and increased research funding to better understand and treat eating disorders. It works with partners and volunteers to develop programs and tools to help everyone who seeks assistance. The organization's website offers toolkits aimed at specific audiences, such as educators, parents, and teens, that contain information on a variety of issues surrounding eating disorders.

National Institute on Drug Abuse (NIDA)

6001 Executive Blvd., Suite 5274, Bethesda, MD   20892-9561
(301) 443-6480 • fax: (301) 443-9127
e-mail: information@nida.nih.gov
website: www.drugabuse.gov

NIDA, a division of the National Institutes of Health, seeks to bring the power of science to bear on drug abuse and addiction. Its goal is to use strategic support and conduct research across a broad range of disciplines, while ensuring the rapid and effective dissemination and use of the results of that research to significantly improve prevention and treatment, and to inform policy as it relates to drug abuse and addiction. Its website contains reports and links directed toward a variety of audiences, including teens, parents, healthcare professionals, and schools.

Office of Juvenile Justice and Delinquency Prevention (OJJDP)

810 Seventh St. NW, Washington, DC   20531
(202) 307-5911
website: www.ojjdp.gov

The Office of Juvenile Justice and Delinquency Prevention provides national leadership, coordination, and resources to prevent and respond to juvenile delinquency and victimization. OJJDP supports states and communities in their efforts to develop and implement effective and coordinated prevention and intervention programs and to improve the juvenile justice system so that it protects public safety, holds offenders accountable, and provides treatment and rehabilitative services tailored to the needs of juveniles and their families. Research on a variety of topics affecting the well-being of young people can be found on its website, including a bulletin analyzing how intervention techniques can lead to different results with girls than with boys.

The Sentencing Project

1705 DeSales St. NW, 8th Floor, Washington, DC   20036
(202) 628-0871 • fax: (202) 628-1091
e-mail: staff@sentencingproject.org
website: www.sentencingproject.org

The Sentencing Project works for a fair and effective US criminal justice system by promoting reforms in sentencing policy, addressing unjust racial disparities and practices, and advocating for alternatives to incarceration. Its work in the area of juvenile justice draws attention to the shift in response to at-risk youth away from providing prevention, protection, and redirection, to tougher sanctions and adult-type punishments instead.

Southern Poverty Law Center

400 Washington Ave., Montgomery, AL   36104
(334) 956-8200
website: www.splcenter.org

The Southern Poverty Law Center is a nonprofit civil rights organization dedicated to fighting hate and bigotry, and to seeking justice for the most vulnerable members of society. One of the center's current priorities is children at risk. The center investigates and reports on the plight of these vulnerable children—disproportionately black and often suffering from learning disabilities—who are being needlessly pushed out of schools and into the juvenile justice system.

Bibliography

Books

Gary Ferguson — *Shouting at the Sky: Troubled Teens and the Promise of the Wild.* New York: St. Martin's Press, 1999.

Sheila Himmel — *Hungry: A Mother and Daughter Fight Anorexia.* New York: Berkeley Trade, 2009.

John Hubner — *Last Chance in Texas: The Redemption of Criminal Youth.* New York: Random House, 2008.

Victor M. Rios — *Punished: Policing the Lives of Black and Latino Boys.* New York: NYU Press, 2011.

Avis Rumney — *Dying to Please: Anorexia, Treatment and Recovery.* Jefferson, NC: McFarland, 2009.

Elizabeth S. Scott and Laurence Steinberg — *Rethinking Juvenile Justice.* Cambridge, MA: Harvard University Press, 2010.

Maia Szalavitz — *Help at Any Cost: How the Troubled-Teen Industry Cons Parents and Hurts Kids.* New York: Riverhead Hardcover, 2006.

Periodicals and Internet Sources

Associated Press | "Police Will Investigate Possible Child Abuse at Youth Boot Camp After Video Goes Viral," *Lubbock-Avalanche Journal*, October 29, 2011.

Kelsey Auman | "One Teen's Story of Breaking Free from Addiction," *The Buffalo News*, May 10, 2012.

Judy Battle | "Not 'Little Adults'—Substance Abuse Treatment for Teens," *Salon*, March 21, 2009. www.salon.com.

James Careless | "Teen Takes Charge in Weight Loss Battle," Canada.com, March 30, 2011. www.o.canada.com.

Brian Charles | "Politicians Hedge on Boot Camps Regulations," *Pasadena Star-News*, November 26, 2011.

John Gorenfeld | "No More Nightmares at Tranquility Bay?" *AlterNet*, January 23, 2006. www.alternet.org.

Kathryn Joyce | "Horror Stories from Tough-Love Teen Homes," *Mother Jones*, July/August 2011.

Craig R. McCoy and John Sullivan | "Center's Abuses Didn't Deter DHS," Philly.com, August 21, 2007. www.philly.com.

Martha Moore | "States Making Juvenile Detention More Localized," *USA Today*, March 16, 2011.

New York Times   "Two Words: Wasteful and
                     Ineffective," October 10, 2010.

Andrew Pollack   "Eating Disorders a New Front in
                     Insurance Fight," *New York Times*,
                     October 13, 2011.

Alina Saminsky   "Preventing Juvenile Delinquency:
                     Early Intervention and
                     Comprehensiveness as Critical
                     Factors," *Student Pulse*, vol. 2, iss. 2,
                     2010. www.studentpulse.com.

Scoop Independent "Boot Camps No More Than
News   'Correctional Quackery,'" February
                     17, 2009. www.scoop.co.nz.

Maia Szalavitz   "Economy Killing Abusive Teen
                     Programs," *Mother Jones*, January 30,
                     2009.

Maia Szalavitz   "New Efforts to Crack Down on
                     Residential Programs for Troubled
                     Teens," *TIME*, October 7, 2011.

Denise Oliver   "Billion Dollar GEO Prison-for-Profit
Velez   Group Abandons Its Mississippi
                     'Cesspool,'" *Daily Kos*, April 29, 2012.
                     www.dailykos.com.

Vicki Veltri   "Time to Enforce Mental Health
                     Parity," *Connecticut News Junkie*,
                     March 18, 2012.

Nancy   "Marketing of Youth Boot Camps
Zuckerbrod   Under Investigation," *USA Today*,
                     April 5, 2008.

Index